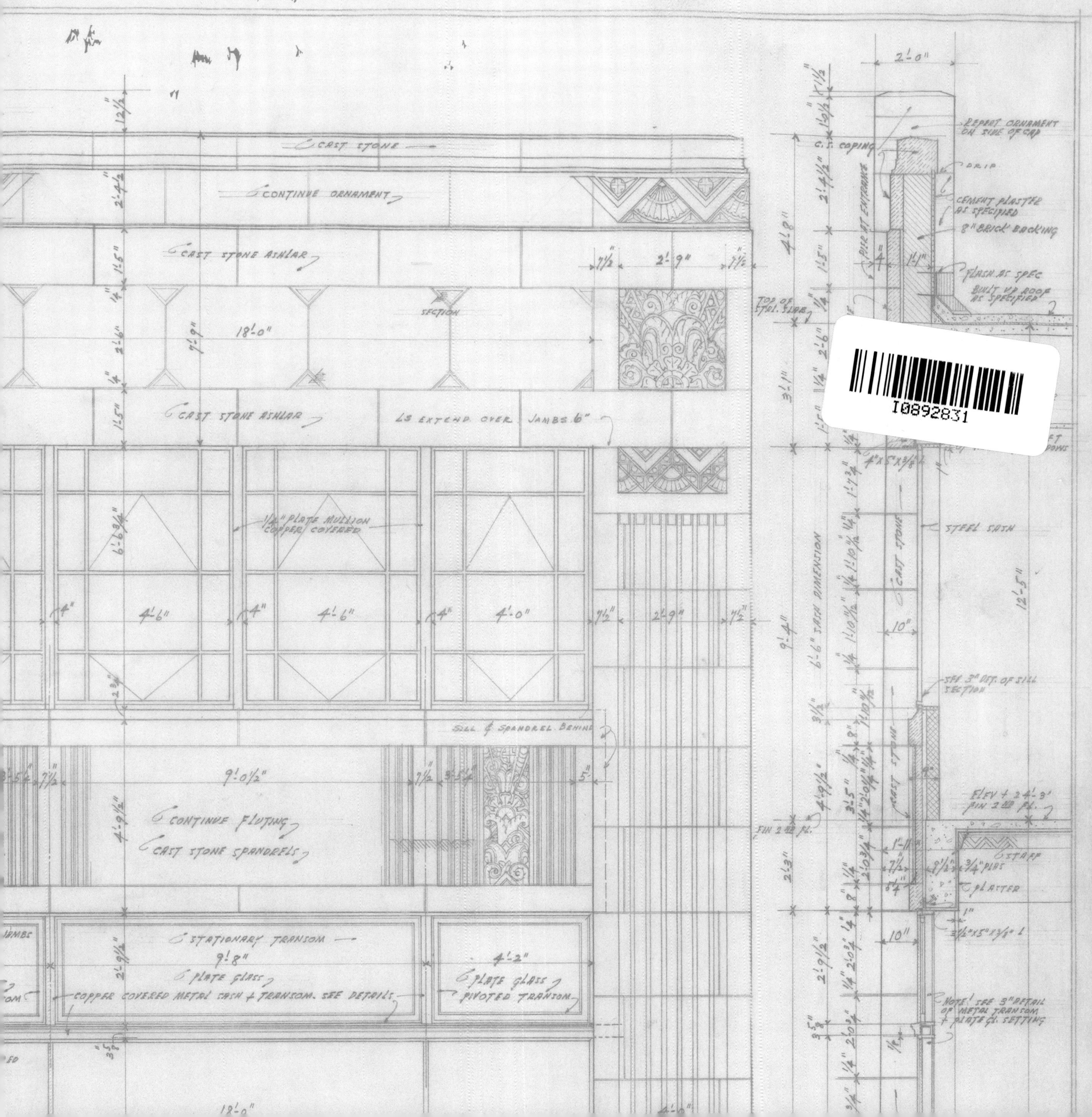
CAST STONE
CONTINUE ORNAMENT
CAST STONE ASHLAR
SECTION
18'-0"
CAST STONE ASHLAR
LS EXTEND OVER JAMBS 6"
1/4" PLATE MULLION COPPER COVERED
4'-6"
4'-6"
4'-0"
2'-9"
SILL & SPANDREL BEHIND
9'-0 1/2"
CONTINUE FLUTING
CAST STONE SPANDRELS
STATIONARY TRANSOM
9'-8"
PLATE GLASS
4'-2"
PLATE GLASS
PIVOTED TRANSOM
COPPER COVERED METAL SASH & TRANSOM. SEE DETAILS
18'-0"
2'-0"
REPEAT ORNAMENT ON SIDE OF CAP
C.S. COPING
PIER AT ENTRANCE
DRIP
CEMENT PLASTER AS SPECIFIED
8" BRICK BACKING
FLASH. AS SPEC
BUILT UP ROOF AS SPECIFIED
TOP OF STEEL SLAB
STEEL SASH
CAST STONE
6'-6" SASH DIMENSION
12'-5"
SEE 3" DET. OF SILL SECTION
CAST STONE
ELEV + 24'-3" FIN 2ND FL.
FIN 2ND FL.
STAFF
3/4" PLUG
PLASTER
NOTE! SEE 3" DETAIL OF METAL TRANSOM & PLATE GL. SETTING

HILL COUNTRY DECO

Modernistic Architecture of Central Texas

HOWARD

HILL COUNTRY DECO

Modernistic Architecture of Central Texas

David Bush and Jim Parsons
Foreword by Mark Wolfe

TCU Press
Fort Worth, Texas

Library of Congress Cataloging-in-Publication Data

Bush, David, 1957-
Hill Country deco : modernistic architecture of central Texas / David Bush and Jim Parsons ;
foreword by Mark Wolfe.
p. cm.
Includes bibliographical references and index.
ISBN 978-0-87565-413-3 (cloth : alk. paper)
1. Art deco (Architecture)--Texas--Texas Hill Country. 2. Architecture--Texas--Texas Hill Country--
History--20th century. I. Parsons, Jim, 1977- II. Title.
NA730.T52T483 2010
720.9764--dc22
2010003975

This project has been funded in part by a grant from
the Fondren Endowed Preservation Services Fund for Texas
of the National Trust for Historic Preservation.

TCU Press
P. O. Box 298300
Fort Worth, Texas 76129
817.257.7822
http://www.prs.tcu.edu

To order books: 800.826.8911

Book design: www.whittingtonandco.com

Printed in China

(Preceding spread)
Fresco detail, "Cattle Ranch,"
San Antonio's Importance in Texas History
U.S. Post Office
615 East Houston Street, San Antonio
Howard Cook, artist
1939

In memory of Martha Welsh Peterson

(Following page)
Elevation, architectural drawing,
Borden's Creamery
875 East Ashby Place, San Antonio
Atlee B. & Robert M. Ayres, architects
1933

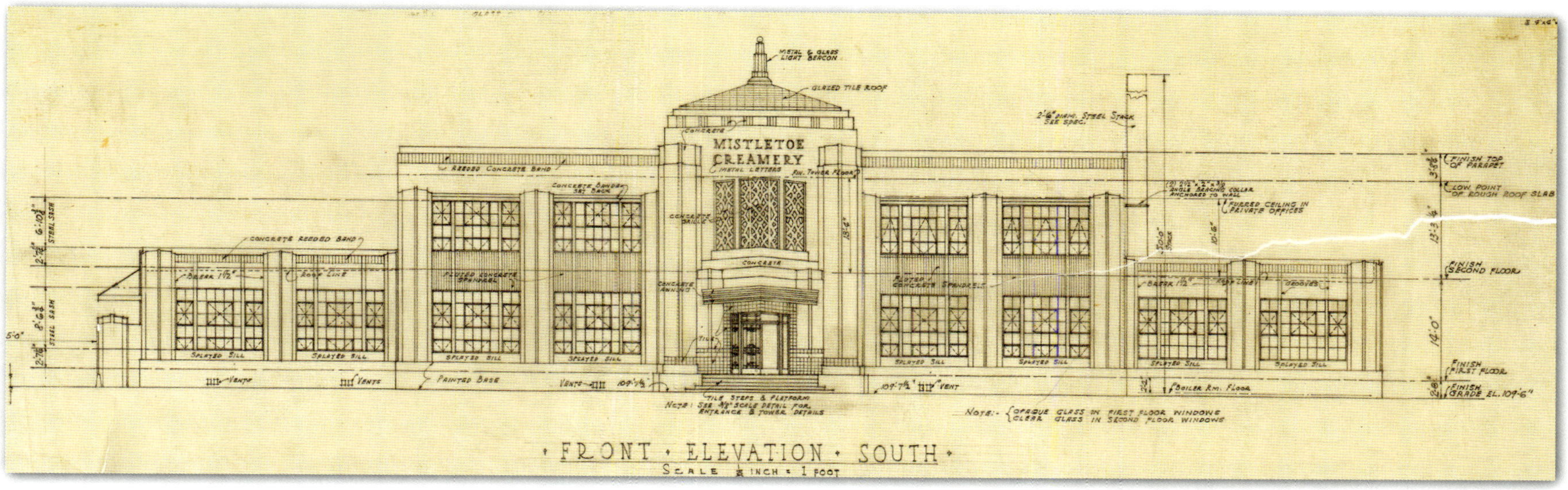

CONTENTS

FOREWORD

C&S Sporting Goods
2120 Guadalupe Street, Austin
Hugo F. Kuehne, architect
1931

2120 Guadalupe Street, shown 2009.

Before World War I, Texans embraced Victorian-era architecture with a vengeance. County courthouses across the state illustrate the depth of the passion Texans had for the most complicated architectural styles imaginable. Rooflines soar in every possible configuration, with arches and columns and eagles scattered like confetti at a parade. Turrets and spires, stained glass, brick and stone mixed in imaginative ways; late nineteenth-century architecture could be fantastical. But after the war, those ornate buildings began to look "old fashioned" and by the late 1920s architects started integrating new, stylish aesthetics imported from Europe. Enter the Art Deco.

It must have seemed very unusual to people accustomed to exuberant Victorian styles. In comparison, Art Deco buildings were smooth, more symmetrical, far simpler in shape and plan, and maybe just a bit too modern for some. More like that new refrigerator in the kitchen than a building should be. But soon it was "out with the old and in with the new," and within a decade excellent examples of Art Deco architecture could be found throughout the state.

The Hill Country was especially well suited for the Art Deco style of the 1920s, '30s and '40s. The traditional agricultural economy was being reshaped by expansive oil discoveries that fed on the upswing in automobile use. The state's strong political connections to Washington through Texas-born Vice President John Nance Garner and others led to a wealth of PWA, WPA, and CCC projects. The state was preparing to celebrate the centennial of its independence from Mexico. And just a few inches below the surface lay an expanse of brilliant white limestone, fine grained and easy to carve, but sturdy and resilient. It was the building material of choice for the Art Deco style.

From county courthouses and banks to gas stations and movie theaters, Art Deco buildings sprang up everywhere. And fortunately many examples survive. In Austin, we have the Travis County Courthouse, a beautiful monument made primarily of locally quarried limestone. For a shining example of the murals that often accompanied such buildings I would direct you to the lobby of Austin's State Highway Building, although many small town post offices sport murals just as impressive.

Unfortunately, the simplicity of Art Deco buildings has also made it easy for insensitive owners to destroy them. A simple layer of stucco can eradicate the beauty of an Art Deco monument in a single afternoon. No special skill is required. Just a failure to recognize true beauty when one sees it, and an account at the local building supply store. Compare, for example, the historic view of the commercial building at 2120 Guadalupe in Austin with the current view of the same building. But just a few steps away, at 2404 Guadalupe, the opposite is true. A Deco façade, almost obliterated by an insensitive remodeling, has been lovingly restored. It's a great example for others to follow.

The International Style came hot on the heels of the Art Deco. For those who thought that Art Deco was restrained, the International Style must have been a rude awakening. Gone were the decorative bas-relief panels and zigzag detailing of the Art Deco, replaced by solid flat undecorated walls and plate glass. If Art Deco buildings were too like the family's refrigerator, then International Style buildings were akin to the chest freezer out in the garage.

In this book, you will find one transitional example of Art Moderne/Streamline style as it phased into the International Style. The former King's Texaco is one of the last remaining intact service stations patterned after a prototype designed by Walter Dorwin Teague, one of the world's most famous industrial designers. It survives today only because the King family refused to let the corporate headquarters dictate alterations that would have destroyed their family's building. It was just too important for that.

These are just a few examples, and there are many more inside. Exciting adventures await you at every turn of the page. And I hope that you won't just look at the pictures and consider your tour complete. Get in your car and drive to these places. If they house functioning businesses, have lunch there, take in a movie, buy some gas, do some shopping, or at very least go inside and tell the people working there how lucky they are to be housed in such a lovely building. Ask them what they know about it, and let them tell you the stories that will bring the building to life. Real places telling real stories; that's what preservation is all about.

So go ahead and get started. There's a lot to see, and you won't want to miss a thing.

Mark Wolfe
Executive Director
Texas Historical Commission
Austin

2404 Guadalupe Street (The Bazaar), Austin
Completed 1937, shown ca.1988

2404 Guadalupe Street, shown 2009.

Mural, State Highway Building (1933), Austin
Harold E. "Bubi" Jessen and Charles E. Milhouse, artists

Karotkin Furniture Co.
217 West Commerce Street, San Antonio
Atlee B. & Robert M. Ayres, architects
1939 (remodel)
In 2003, new owners returned the Karotkin building to its ca. 1900 appearance.

INTRODUCTION

"Is modernistic architecture soon to replace the prevailing styles? Do Colonial, Elizabethan, Italian Renaissance now belong to the past in this country . . . shall we soon refer to them with the complacent superiority with which we mention Victorian Gothic, French Mansard, Cupola and Band Saw architecture?"

William Orr Ludlow
Fellow, American Institute of Architects
San Antonio Express
September 28, 1930

"The entire personnel of Karotkin Furniture Company is proud of its new store and welcomes this opportunity of showing Mr. and Mrs. San Antonio 'the furniture store of tomorrow' designed for the shopper of today."

San Antonio Sunday Light
November 12, 1939

Despite being the architecture of the Jazz Age and aerodynamic design, Art Deco, like Karotkin's store of tomorrow, was never completely new. Behind the modernist trappings it was as referential, if not reverential, as the revival styles that went before it.

For architects trained in the late nineteenth and early twentieth centuries, Art Deco offered a new way of interpreting classical architecture. Art Deco not only translated Roman and Greek detailing into a modern idiom, it integrated Gothic ornamentation with mechanical precision, gave Art Nouveau's flowing forms an angular edge, and borrowed freely from three great pyramid-building cultures—the Egyptians, Mayans and Aztecs. In Central Texas, the architecture of San Antonio's colonial missions also provided a significant source of inspiration.

Art Deco designers can even be considered heirs to the Arts and Crafts Movement. Although modernistic construction required mass-produced materials such as concrete, steel, and glass block, the work of craftsmen and artisans was equally important. Despite its celebration of mechanization and modernization, Art Deco was in many ways the last hurrah for traditional architectural ornamentation before it was swept away in the post World War II tidal wave of the International Style.

DECO DEFINED

Art Deco generally refers to the dominant design movement in the United States from the mid-1920s through 1940, although the late 1920s to 1950 is a more accurate period of influence in Texas. The term Art Deco was not used when these buildings were constructed; at the time the style was referred to as "modernistic" or simply "modern" design. British art historian and author Bevis Hillier coined the expression Art Deco in the late 1960s when the style was being rediscovered after decades of disdain. Hillier adapted the name from the 1925 Exposition des Arts Décoratifs et Industriels Modernes, the Parisian trade fair instrumental in promoting the popularity of modernistic design.

Art Deco is a fairly generic term that has come to mean many things to many people. Its imprecision is evident in the number of names applied to the style and the three major subsets of modernistic design.

ART DECO

Art Deco is the classic modernistic design of the 1920s and early 1930s. It is sometimes called Zigzag Deco or Zigzag Moderne for its distinctive angular detailing. Buildings in this style are highly ornamented with geometric interpretations of natural forms or stylized examples of ancient and classical architectural ornamentation. These buildings usually have symmetrical façades, are vertically oriented, and frequently include pylons or towers that emphasize the building's height. Highly ornamented metalwork is common, particularly around entrances and store windows. Interior decoration frequently includes elaborate grilles and banisters, colorful murals, and polished stone. Pyramidal or stepped roofs with lanterns, beacons or pinnacles are characteristic of Art Deco design especially on the stepped-back skyscrapers of the period. The style is generally found on urban commercial buildings and some public buildings designed before the onset of the Great Depression.

Egyptian Revival capital, Memorial Amphitheater, 1937, Gonzales.

Relief, Blum's, 1930, San Antonio.

ART MODERNE

The architecture usually associated with 1930s Fred Astaire and Ginger Rogers musicals is sometimes called Streamline Deco or Streamline Moderne for its sweeping curves. Art Moderne was inspired by industrial design, particularly the era's new airliners, ocean liners, and aerodynamic automobiles. Ornamentation is very restrained, especially when compared to 1920s Art Deco buildings. Stucco is commonly used to create smooth exterior wall surfaces; lines incised into the stucco suggest architectural elements, such as columns and cornices. Art Moderne buildings are usually asymmetrical with a horizontal orientation, flat roofs, and at least one rounded corner. Casement windows are often continuous around corners. Glass block and round windows are also common. Art Moderne is usually found on suburban commercial buildings and the relatively few modernistic houses built in the 1930s.

WPA DECO

WPA Deco is the result of two frequently competing influences: changing architectural tastes and cost concerns. Somewhat derogatively called "starved classicism," this style features simplified classical detailing applied to traditional building forms. It is also sometimes called PWA Deco or PWA Moderne.

The names refer to two major components of President Franklin D. Roosevelt's New Deal. In 1933, Congress authorized the creation of the Public Works Administration to stimulate business and reduce unemployment by funding public works projects. The PWA spent more than six billion dollars on new schools, courthouses, post offices, hospitals, and city halls as well as highways, dams, and transportation systems.

The Works Progress Administration (later renamed the Work Projects Administration) was the largest New Deal agency. The WPA directly employed millions of Americans to construct schools, parks, roads, and public buildings.

Public art is an important component of many PWA and WPA projects. The most familiar examples are the murals painted in large and small post offices across the country. The U. S. Treasury Department's Section of Painting and Sculpture (later the Section of Fine Art) hired artists and selected the themes of the murals with input from the community in which the art would be displayed. The federal government set aside 1 percent of the construction costs for "embellishment" from which the artists were paid.[1]

WPA Deco combines the symmetry and squared angles of Art Deco design with Art Moderne's horizontal orientation, flat roofs, and clean lines. While Art Moderne helped pave the way for the unornamented International Style, WPA Deco was built on the Beaux-Arts tradition. The classically inspired ornamentation is stylized along modernist lines. There is more ornamentation than in Art Moderne design, but not as much as on Art Deco buildings. The style is found on post offices, courthouses, schools, and city halls that were designed and built with federal assistance during the Great Depression.

HILL COUNTRY DECO

Geologically, the Texas Hill Country begins west of Austin and northwest of San Antonio where the Balcones Escarpment separates the rugged limestone of the Edwards Plateau from the more fertile Coastal Plain. This book includes this region as well as counties to the east. Austin and San Antonio architects had the most influence in this region, particularly during the Great Depression, when federal programs funded the construction of modernistic government buildings outside major population centers. At the same time, the state of Texas commemorated the centennial of the Texas Revolution with several ambitious building projects of its own. Because many of the revolution's most significant actions took place in Central Texas, modernistic museums and monuments dot the area.

San Antonio was by far the largest city in the region with a population of almost 232,000 in 1930. Austin was a distant second at about 53,000, and New Braunfels an even more distant third with 6,200 people. Although San Antonio architects designed buildings throughout Central Texas, the city's architecture was very different from that in the surrounding area.

In the 1920s, San Antonio was enjoying expansive growth and the biggest building boom in its history. The population grew by 43 percent between 1920 and 1930, and suburban development pushed the city limits north.[2] By the beginning of November 1929, the local government had issued building permits for a record twenty-five million dollars worth of projects.[3]

Detail, U.S. Court House, 1936, Austin.

(Left)
Streamlined detailing, Dempsey Berryhill house, 1935, San Antonio.

East entrance, Southwestern Bell Telephone and Telegraph Building, 1931, San Antonio.

At the beginning of the boom, the architecture of the moment was Spanish Colonial Revival. It was a big change for a city largely made up of traditional neoclassical and Victorian buildings with a smattering of authentic Spanish Colonial structures. The revival was part of a regional architectural movement popularized by the 1915 Panama-California Exposition in San Diego celebrating the opening of the Panama Canal. Architects designing in this style contrasted plain walls with rich ornamentation exhibiting Mexican, Spanish, and Moorish influences. The style's similarities to the design of San Antonio's historic missions made it an obvious choice both for celebrating local heritage and distinguishing the city from other urban areas.

Two neighboring buildings on Auditorium Plaza in downtown San Antonio illustrate the dynamic changes that impacted local architecture. Although it is the newer of the two, I. H. Timlin's Southwestern Bell Telephone and Telegraph Building is the more traditional design. Finely detailed replicas of Spanish Renaissance ornamentation are applied to an otherwise conventional office building.[4]

Next door, the San Antonio Municipal Auditorium designed by Atlee B. & Robert M. Ayres with George R. Willis and Emmett T. Jackson exhibits modernistic massing and simplified ornamentation described at the time as "modified Spanish."[5]

The detailing on the paired towers is almost streamlined, especially the lines of the stylized volute buttresses. This type of tower would be repeated to great effect in later buildings that incorporated elements of the Spanish Colonial Revival and modernistic design.

Modernistic architecture outside San Antonio is much more in the textbook Art Deco tradition. Descendants of settlers from the American South and Germany dominated the surrounding region and did not share the big city's predilection for Spanish ornamentation. As state capital, Austin supported a robust architectural community that produced sophisticated examples of each of the major subtypes of Art Deco design. By 1939, even though it was a relatively small city, Austin possessed significant modernistic buildings for every level of government from municipal through national.

Art Deco gradually spread to smaller cities and towns in Central Texas by the start of the 1930s. Even though the Depression brought commercial construction to a standstill in many agricultural communities, some surprising modernistic business buildings exist in unexpected places. Nevertheless, federally funded projects produced the bulk of rural Art Deco design. The Hill Country does possess a distinctive architectural heritage in stone construction, but roughhewn modernistic buildings, such as Lampasas Junior High School, are extremely rare.

With the outbreak of World War II and the rationing of building supplies, private construction again ceased. The pent-up demand after the war resulted in an explosion of commercial construction, including a surge of suburban and small-town movie theaters that carried Art Deco and Art Moderne influences through the mid-twentieth century.

Modernistic buildings are found in towns and cities throughout Central Texas. The majority of traditional Art Deco buildings stand in the downtown commercial districts of Austin and San Antonio. Modernistic stores, theaters, and WPA Deco government buildings can be found on or near the main streets of larger towns. The biggest concentrations of automobile-oriented Art Moderne development are along Fredericksburg Road and Broadway, the primary thoroughfares leading to San Antonio's northern suburbs, although a surprising number of historic service stations survive on streets and highways throughout the region. The north side of San Antonio and Austin's Old West End are interspersed with modernistic houses and apartment buildings.

The buildings photographed for this book are grouped according to their original uses: commercial, institutional and residential. Theaters are included in a separate chapter, as are commemorative structures built for the Texas Centennial.

Within each chapter, buildings are listed by their historic names; more familiar names are included where appropriate. To illustrate the evolution and spread of modernistic design across the region, buildings are listed in chronological order based on the date of their completion or when they were remodeled in a modernistic style. Architects, contractors, and completion dates were determined from a variety of sources including cornerstones and plaques, period newspapers, professional journals, architectural drawings, city directories, and telephone directories.

Tower, San Antonio Municipal Auditorium, 1926, San Antonio.

Detail, Lampasas Junior High School, 1938, Lampasas.

KRESS
5-10-25¢ STORE
S. H. KRESS & CO.
5-10-25¢ STORE
KRESS
KRESS
THREE

COMMERCIAL

"*This is a materialistic, scientific and practical age that Jules Verne could not picture with his wildest imagination . . . at last we have a new style, which in a hundred years from now history will record as a distinct and as clearly defined an epoch as any of the past.*"

Harry Allan Jacobs
The New York Times
November 30, 1930

The phrase "dime store" does not usually conjure up the image of a five-story downtown department store with basement cafeteria, in-store ice cream plant, and employee dining room with rooftop patio, but in 1939 that is what S. H. Kress & Company opened on East Houston Street in San Antonio. The store was the largest in the Kress chain following the seven-story flagship operation on Fifth Avenue in New York.[1]

To fulfill company founder Samuel H. Kress' vision, the chain's in-house architectural division created distinctive, individually designed stores that distinguished Kress outlets from other five-and-dimes. The idea was not only popular, it was financially successful. For over twenty years, beginning in 1927, Kress had the highest per-store sales of any variety chain in the country, including those of its larger rivals, Woolworth and Kresge.[2]

Kress staff architect Edward F. Sibbert designed the company's most significant stores during the peak years of the chain's expansion from the end of the Roaring Twenties through the Great Depression to World War II. For the San Antonio store, Sibbert adapted Spanish Colonial architectural details in combination with more traditional Art Deco design elements. Unfortunately, safety netting obscures this unique storefront.

Unlike San Antonio's Kress store, most of the modernistic retail buildings in the Hill Country were not new construction. An industry driven by trends was quick to embrace the new style; the relative ease of installing an updated storefront over an existing façade only made it more popular. By the end of the 1930s, most of the major retailers in San Antonio and Austin had remodeled their downtown stores in Art Deco or Art Moderne style, which also spread to small cities and towns in the region.

With its emphasis on modernity and Machine Age design, Art Deco architecture was ideal for automobile-related businesses such as car dealerships and garages. American oil companies adapted the style when they began standardizing station design in the 1920s. The move coincided with efforts to improve the image of filling stations by upgrading facilities to service stations.

S.H. Kress & Co. 5¢-10¢-25¢ Store
311-315 East Houston Street, San Antonio
Edward F. Sibbert (New York), architect
Ed W. Oeffinger, contractor
1939

Cornice signage, S.H. Kress & Co.

In 1926, San Antonio began a flood control project to eliminate an S-shaped bend in the San Antonio River. The project also connected an undeveloped area known as Bowen's Island to the rest of downtown. Smith Brothers Development awarded Ayres & Ayres the prestigious job of designing the buildings in what was called San Antonio's "new downtown."[3]

Although the Smith-Young Tower's detailing is neo-Gothic, the profile is that of a classic stepped-back skyscraper. It was San Antonio's tallest building until 1988.

Another very different building on Bowen's Island also reflects the influence of exotic styles on Art Deco design. The Moorish-inspired tilework on the Plaza Hotel garage contrasts with the modernistic chevrons. The garage reflects the architectural theme of the nearby Plaza Hotel, now the Granada Homes apartment building.[4]

(Clockwise from left)

Smith-Young Tower, later Transit Tower; Tower Life Building
310 South St. Mary's Street, San Antonio
Atlee B. & Robert M. Ayres, architects
McKenzie Construction Co., contractor
1929

Architectural drawing, Smith-Young Tower.

Plaza Hotel Garage
419 South St. Mary's Street, San Antonio
Atlee B. & Robert M. Ayres, architects
McKenzie Construction Co., contractor
1928

Tilework, Plaza Hotel Garage.

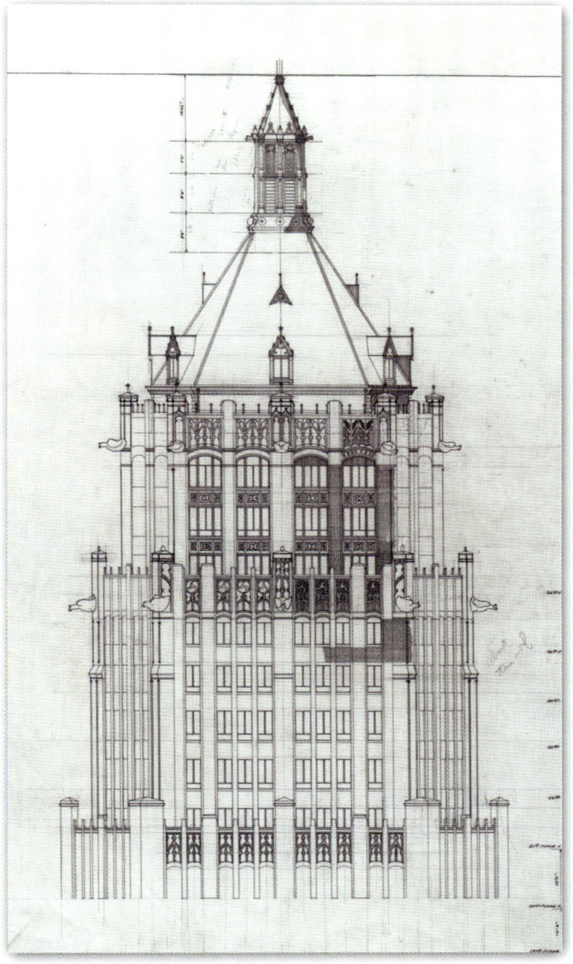

419

HUMBLE
OILS

HUMBLE OIL & REFINING CO.
HUMBLE
OILS
HOUSTON, TEXAS

In the 1920s, Humble Oil hired architect John F. Staub to create a new standard service station to distinguish the company's dealers from traditional filling stations. At the time, Staub was best known for designing large suburban homes for wealthy clients.[5]

It is extremely rare to find one of the Staub Humble stations with its decorative tilework and signage intact.

The condition of the former Wight station, the first of the Humble standard stations built in San Antonio, and the former Tucker station, a smaller standardized version Staub designed, is more typical of surviving Humble stations.[6]

(Opposite page: clockwise from upper left)
Humble Oil Service Station No. 63
1020 South Laredo Street, San Antonio
John F. Staub (Houston), architect
ca. 1928

Tilework, Humble Service Station No. 63.

Signage, Humble Service Station No. 63.

(This page: top)
C. Charley Wight Humble Oil Super Service Station No. 3
926 South Presa Street, San Antonio
1928

H.H. Tucker Humble Oil Service Station
1502 McCullough Avenue, San Antonio
c. 1930

Van Horn Drug Store No. 1
2520 McCullough Avenue, San Antonio
ca. 1928

Great Atlantic & Pacific Tea Co. Store No. 177
2500 North Main Avenue, San Antonio
1929

Detail, A&P Store No. 177, San Antonio.

Packard Motor Car Co. manufactured luxury automobiles. The company's distinctive, individually designed showrooms were one of its trademarks.[7]

Gene Meador Packard
1123 North Main Avenue, San Antonio
Atlee B. & Robert M. Ayres, architects
1929

Detail, Gene Meador Packard.

AVENUE E
THIRD
BIKE LANE
AHEAD

The *San Antonio Express* and *San Antonio Evening News* officially opened their new building on October 29, 1929, "Black Tuesday," the day of the stock market crash that signaled the start of the Great Depression.[8]

Pompeo Coppini created the sculpture "Enlightening of the Press" for installation above the building's entrance. The work features telephone and telegraph lines spanning the globe and six allegorical figures representing Labor, Education, Knowledge, Enlightenment, and Justice. Knowledge points to Texas (some say San Antonio) on the globe.[9]

For the Express News Building lobby, San Antonio artist José Arpa created a series of murals tracing the creation of a newspaper from the forest to the reader. Unfortunately, most of the murals were installed behind pillars in the corners of the lobby where they cannot be photographed.[10]

(Opposite page)
Express News Building
Third Street and Avenue E, San Antonio
Herbert S. Green, architect
Jopling Construction Co. (Dallas), contractor
1929

(This Page: clockwise from top left)
Detail, Express News Building

Lobby, Express News Building

Lobby details, Express News Building

"Enlightening of the Press"
Express News Building, Pompeo Coppini, sculptor.

When Alamo National Bank commissioned Graham, Anderson, Probst & White to design its new building, the architecture firm was already nationally known. The architects had designed Chicago's Wrigley Building, Merchandise Mart and Shedd Aquarium, among many other projects.

San Antonio artist Ruth Dunn created the Alamo in stained glass, which was in-

stalled over the building's Commerce Street entrance in 1964.[11]

In 1993, set decorators installed the Art Deco-inspired oil paintings, "Trust" and "Thrift," in the banking hall for the filming of the movie *Blank Check*.[12]

(Opposite page, clockwise)
Alamo National Building, later Drury Plaza Hotel
105 South St. Mary's Street, San Antonio
Graham, Anderson, Probst & White (Chicago), architects
1930

Paintings, banking hall, Alamo National Building.

Detail, Alamo National Building.

(Left) Capital, banking hall, Alamo National Building.

(Below) Banking hall, Alamo National Building.

Emil Blum opened his first dry goods store in 1908 after managing other San Antonio stores and training in Chicago and Houston. In 1929, Blum's, Inc. announced an extensive project to remodel the Princess Theater (1912) into a chic department store. The new store opened to great fanfare in 1930, but Blum's declared bankruptcy within seven months. Frost Bros., at that time a women's specialty store, moved into the building in 1931 and operated there until 1988.[13]

Blum's, later Frost Bros.
217 East Houston Street, San Antonio
Harvey L. Page with Ralph H. Cameron, architects
Jim Westerhof, contractor
1930 (remodel)

Details, Blum's.

FROST'S
FROST BROS
FROST BROS

The remodeling of Austin National Bank's 1910 building resulted in an unusual combination of traditional neoclassical design within an Egyptian Deco vault. After World War II, the bank expanded and remodeled its building in a more streamlined style. Research indicates that either C. H. Page & Son or Page, Southerland & Page, designed the 1948 project.[14]

Austin National Bank, demolished
507 Congress Avenue, Austin
Page Brothers, architects
1930 (remodel)

Interior, Austin National Bank, shown 1930.

Façade after expansion and remodeling, Austin National Bank, shown ca. 1948. This building was demolished ca. 1960.

Texas Power & Light Building
407 North Main Street, Taylor
1930 (remodel)

Transom, Texas Power & Light Building.

Chapline Building
1701 Guadalupe Street, Austin
Roy L. Thomas, architect
Scott Yeamans, contractor
1930

Detail, Chapline Building.

Central Power & Light Building
502 St. Paul Street, Gonzales
John M. Marriott, architect
1930

Capital, Central Power & Light Building.

Cornice detail, Central Power & Light Building.

Mutual Deposit & Loan Co./Fidelity Mortgage Co., later Nelsen Partners
905 Congress Avenue, Austin
Hugo F. Kuehne, architect
1930 (remodel)

Detail, Mutual Deposit & Loan Co.

Relief, Mutual Deposit & Loan Co.

NelsenPartners

FIRST NATIONAL
BANK
FIRST NATIONAL BANK

First National Bank of New Braunfels, demolished
111 West San Antonio Street, New Braunfels
Giesecke & Harris with Jeremiah Schmidt, architects
Walsh, Burney & Key, contractor
1931

E.Y. White, Inc. Laundry, Cleaning, Dyeing and Storage
110 West Josephine Street, San Antonio
1931

Detail, E.Y. White Laundry.

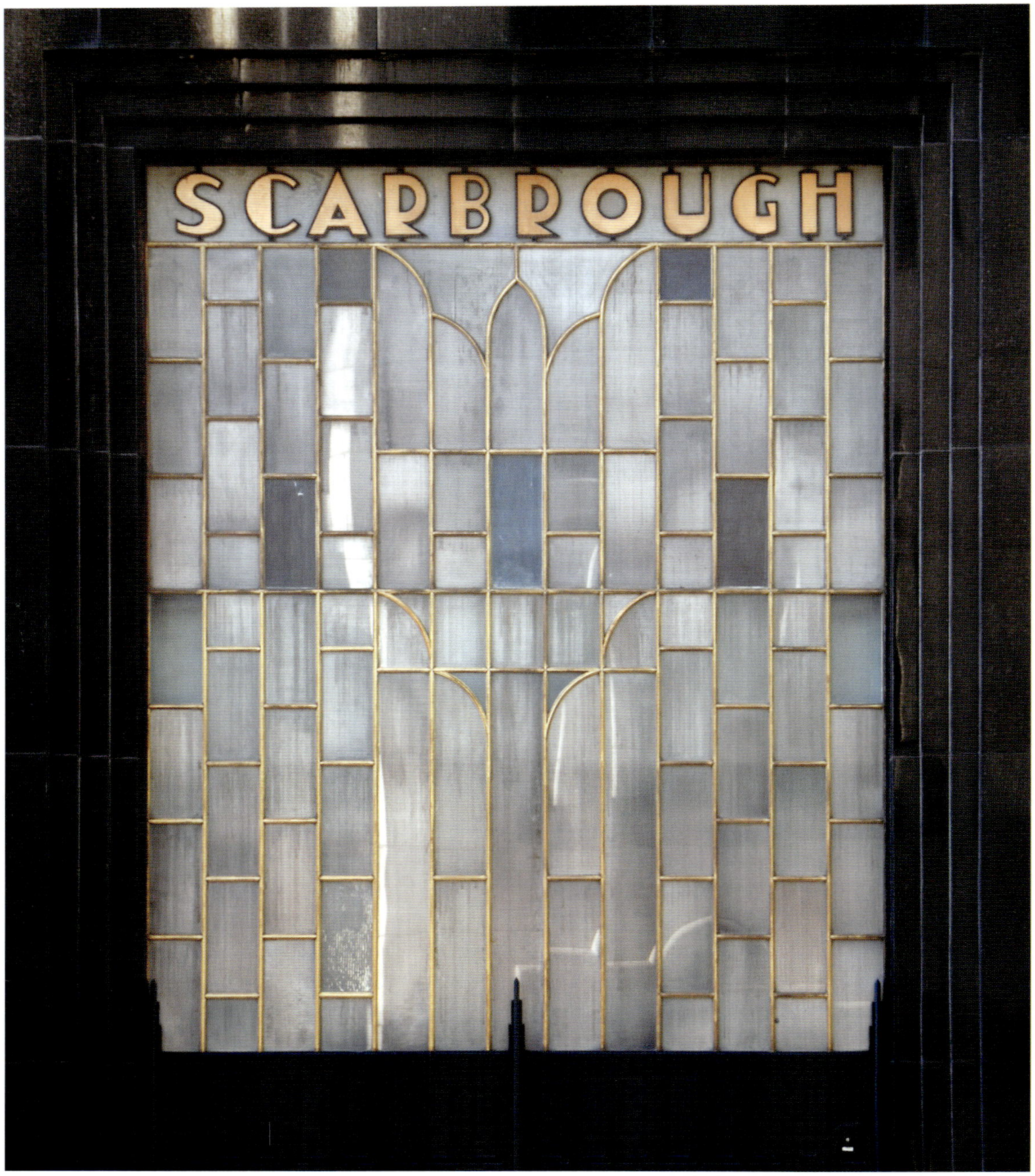

In 1910, Emerson Monroe Scarbrough built Austin's first skyscraper adjacent to his Congress Avenue mercantile store. Twenty years later, the Scarbrough company expanded and updated the six-story building in the Art Deco style and built a modernistic wing to replace the original store. Scarbrough's downtown department store closed in 1983.[15]

(Clockwise from upper left)

Scarbrough's
101 West Sixth Street, Austin
Wyatt C. Hedrick (Fort Worth) and Edwin C. Kreisle, architects
James F. Taylor (Fort Worth), contractor
1931 (remodel)

Detail, Scarbrough's.

Congress Avenue entrance, Scarbrough's.

Sixth Street entrance detail, Scarbrough's.

THE FAIR
JACCARD
QUALITY
RAZOR-BLADES
FACTORY-PRICES

Grand-Silver, a national chain of 5¢ to 25¢ stores, constructed this building and occupied most of the first floor. Jaccard Millinery Store leased the remainder of the first floor and all of the second floor.[16]

F. W. Grand-Silver Store, later The Palm Restaurant
233 East Houston Street, San Antonio
1931

Detail, Grand-Silver Store

(Opposite)
Jaccard Millinery Store
225 East Houston Street, San Antonio
Shown ca. 1931

LEO MENDLOVITZ
SUMMER GOODS

It is very likely Jeremiah Schmidt designed the remodeling of the Mendlovitz store in New Braunfels. He had designed the Mendlovitz home in Seguin in 1930 and was the architect for the remodeling of the Mendlovitz Seguin store at the same time the dry goods company remodeled its New Braunfels store.[17]

Leo Mendlovitz Department Store
214 West San Antonio Street, New Braunfels
Jeremiah Schmidt, architect, attributed
1932 (remodel)

214 West San Antonio Street, shown 2009.

(Clockwise from bottom of this page)

Woodlawn Telephone Exchange

110 Warner Avenue, San Antonio

I.R. Timlin (St. Louis), architect

1932

Cornice detail, Woodlawn Telephone Exchange.

Entrance, Woodlawn Telephone Exchange.

Detail, Woodlawn Telephone Exchange

Lantern, Woodlawn Telephone Exchange.

110

Mistletoe Creameries commissioned Atlee B. & Robert M. Ayres to design its new plant. Mistletoe became part of the Borden Co. during construction and the facility opened as Borden's Creamery. Ayres & Ayres designed significant additions and alterations to the building in 1946, 1948, 1952, 1965, and 1964.[18]

Borden's Creamery, later Arrington's Star Storage
875 East Ashby Place, San Antonio
Atlee B. & Robert M. Ayres, architects
King B. Key, contractor
1933

Elevation, architectural drawing, Borden's Creamery

Lantern, Borden's Creamery.

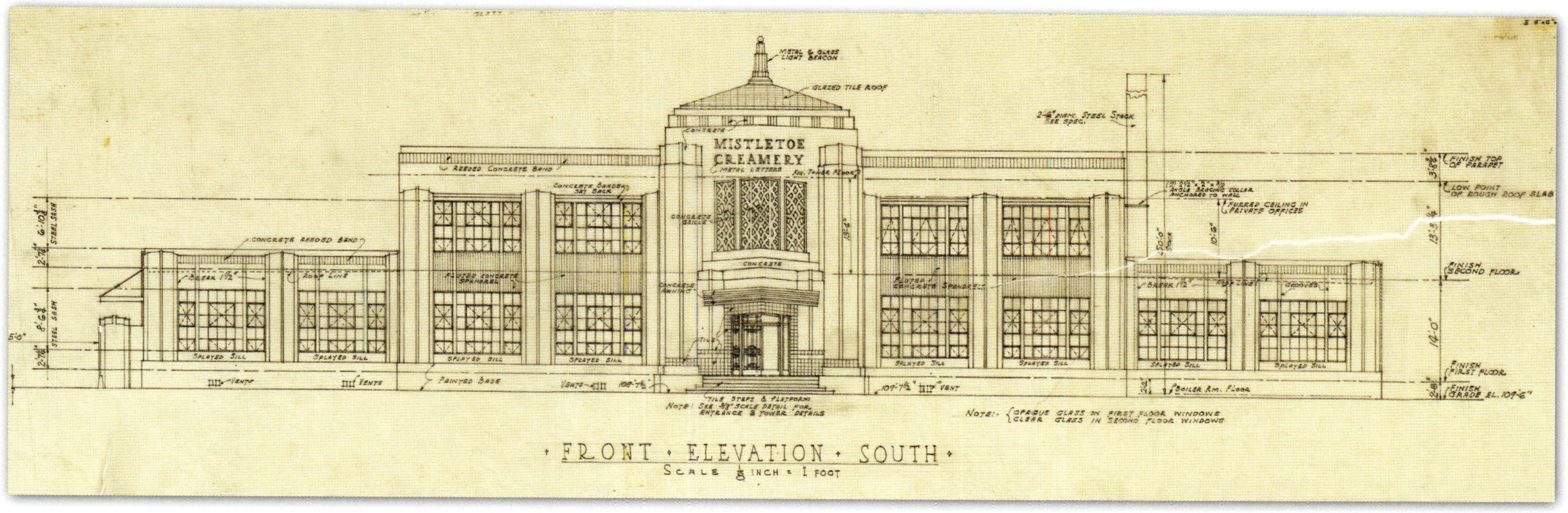
MISTLETOE
CREAMERY
FRONT · ELEVATION · SOUTH

Edward Stein was president of Fredericksburg National Bank when he designed the bank's new building.[19]

Fredericksburg National Bank, later Showcase Antiques
119 East Main Street, Fredericksburg
Edward Stein, architect
1936

Entrance, Fredericksburg National Bank.

Monogram, Fredericksburg National Bank.

SHOWCASE
ANTIQUES
Double Fudge

the mix
the mix
2423

Suburban shopping centers were called community centers when the concept was first developed. The Fulton Community Center *(left)* originally occupied most of the 1700 block of Fredericksburg Road extending south from Fulton Avenue. Some sections have been demolished and others significantly altered.[20]

(Left)
Fulton Community Center
1720-1722 Fredericksburg Road, San Antonio
1936 (remodel)

(Below)
Pease Veterinary Hospital, later South Congress Veterinary Clinic
3300 South Congress Avenue, Austin
1936

(Opposite)
Hom-Ond, pronounced "home-owned," Food Store No. 1
2423 North St. Mary's Street, San Antonio
Max M. Sandfield, architect
Banspach Brothers, contractor
1935

SCHREINER

Schreiner Cash Food Store
224 Earl Garrett Street, Kerrville
Adams & Adams, architects
Bruno Schott, contractor
1936

Detail, Schreiner Cash Food Store.

Cavin Filling Station, later Gomez Tire Shop
2018 Roosevelt Avenue, San Antonio
ca. 1937

Chas. Schreiner Co. built the food store as an annex to its existing department store. Shreiner's opened as a general mercantile store in 1869 and operated continuously until 2007.[21]

Guaranty State Bank, partially demolished
Main Plaza, New Braunfels
Phelps & Dewees with Jeremiah Schmidt, architects
1937 (remodel)

Façade, Guaranty State Bank.

Detail, Guaranty State Bank.

Ebensberger Funeral Home
later Ebensberger-Fisher Funeral Home
111 Rosewood Avenue, Boerne
Adams & Adams, architects
1938

Door, Ebensberger Funeral Home.

Detail, Ebensberger Funeral Home.

In 1944, a new owner renamed the business Olmos Pharmacy for its location in the Olmos Park neighborhood. "Olmos" has been misspelled on the clock since the name was changed.[22]

Gilmore Pharmacy
later Olmos Pharmacy, Olmos Bharmacy
3902 McCullough Avenue, San Antonio
1938

Businessman Herman Brown commissioned this building as the Austin headquarters for his holdings, including what was then the Brown & Root construction company.[23]

Brown Building
710 Colorado Street, Austin
C.H. Page & Son, architects
1938

Entrance, Brown Building.

Golden West Master Service Station No. 5,
later Freddy's Mexican Restaurant
1201 South Flores Street, San Antonio
1939

Frank Bros., later Fuddruckers
115 Alamo Plaza, San Antonio
Atlee B. & Robert M. Ayres, architects
1939 (remodel)

The Ayres design of the Frank Bros. store has been altered with the installation of windows across the second floor; the openings in the two end bays were originally covered with frosted glass and illuminated from behind. Frank Bros. specialized in menswear, military uniforms, and school uniforms. The company's downtown store operated at this location from 1914 to 1983.[24]

RIVERCENTER

Joske Bros. built a new department store on the corner of East Commerce Street and Alamo Plaza in 1887 and added two floors to the building in 1909. The modernistic façade encloses the historic building and the 1939 expansion promoted as, "The Biggest Store in the Biggest State." The business operated under the Joske's name until 1987.[25]

Joske's, later Dillard's
100 Alamo Plaza, San Antonio
Bartlett Cocke, architect
Walsh & Burney Co., contractor
1939 (remodel)

Details, Joske's.

Sammie's Place, later Hut's Hamburgers
807 West Sixth Street, Austin
1939

Taylor Motor Co.
200 Porter Street, Taylor
ca. 1940

SUPER
CHEVROLET
SERVICE
TAYLOR MOTOR CO.
AUTO CREDIT
SERVICE ★ CENTER
"WE SERVICE WHAT WE SELL!"

In 1939, multi-millionaire oilman James M. West founded the *Austin Daily Tribune* to advance his personal political agenda. The *Tribune* provided unwavering support for West's friend Governor W. Lee "Pappy" O'Daniel and other allies, coupled with unbridled criticism of President Franklin D. Roosevelt and his administration. The short-lived afternoon paper was published from October 1, 1939 to December 29, 1942. West died four months after opening the modernistic Tribune building; his sons closed the newspaper a year later. The State of Texas bought the building in 1945.[26]

Austin Daily Tribune Building,
later Ernest O. Thompson State Office Building
920 Colorado Street, Austin
Shirley Simons, Sr. and Page, Southerland & Page, architects
1941

Greek key detail, Austin Daily Tribune Building.

Corner detail, Austin Daily Tribune Building.

DETOUR
920

EARL ABEL'S
OUR OWN BAKERY
OPEN 24 HOURS
"Is everything alright?"
GOOD FOODS
4210

When Earl Abel's opened, the drive-in restaurant had $8,000 worth of neon lights, indoor seating for 125 people and parking for 150 cars.[27]

Earl Abel's Super-Drive-In, demolished
4120 Broadway, San Antonio
Lloyd Shoop, architect
Howard Bumbaugh, contractor
1941

San Antonio Conservation Society restored the Deason building's modernistic façade in 2006.

Deason Radio Co.
102 Navarro Street, San Antonio
G.M. Becher, architect
1941 (remodel)

Door handle, Deason Radio Co.

Richter's produced Butter-Krust bread at this plant from 1941 to 1997. The company expanded the building in 1948, 1956, and 1966.[28]

Richter's Bakery
2203 Broadway, San Antonio
Charles T. Boelhauwe, architect
1941

Brickwork, Richter's Bakery.

Detail, Richter's Bakery.

Scheffler Service Station
6421 Broadway, Alamo Heights
1941

Detail, Scheffler Service Station.

F.A. Menger Electric Co.
1424 Fredericksburg Road, San Antonio
1946

General Neon Advertising Co., demolished
101 Lexington Avenue, San Antonio
1946

Guaranty Finance Co., later Miller Blueprint
501 West Sixth Street, Austin
Roy L. Thomas, architect
1946

Entrance, Guaranty Finance Co.

Detail, Guaranty Finance Co.

Company founder Victor Stanzel designed the front office section of his model airplane factory.

Victor Stanzel Co.
1201 Kessler Avenue, Schulenberg
1946

Neisner Bros. was a national chain of 5¢ to $1 stores. The openings in the façade were originally covered in frosted glass illuminated from behind. In 2009, additional floors were added to the building when it was converted into a hotel.[29]

(Opposite)
Neisner's, later TownePlace Suites
409 East Houston Street, San Antonio
Atlee B. & Robert M. Ayres, architects
1947

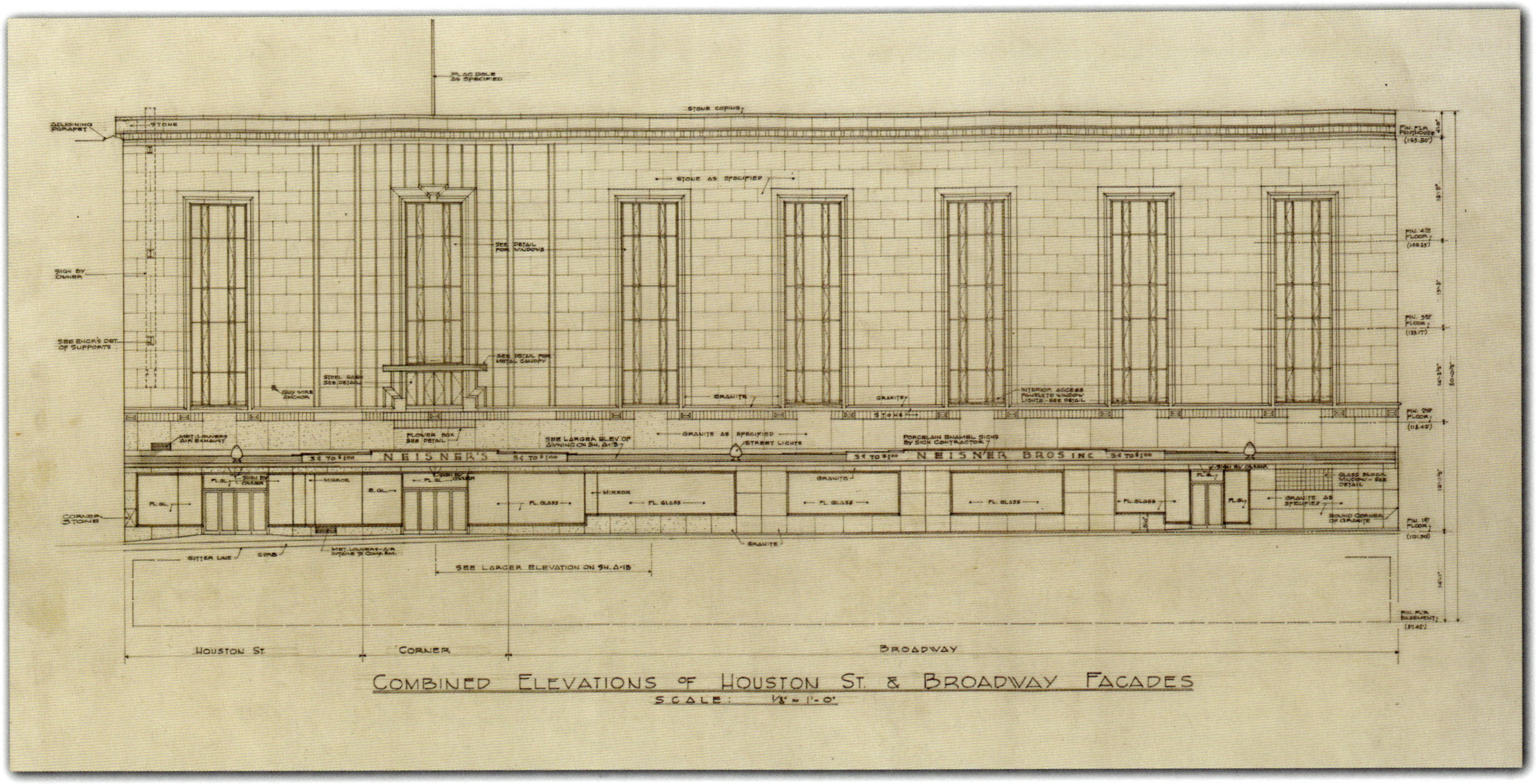

Elevation, architectural drawing, Neisner's.

This signage design was apparently rejected and was not used on the Neisner store.

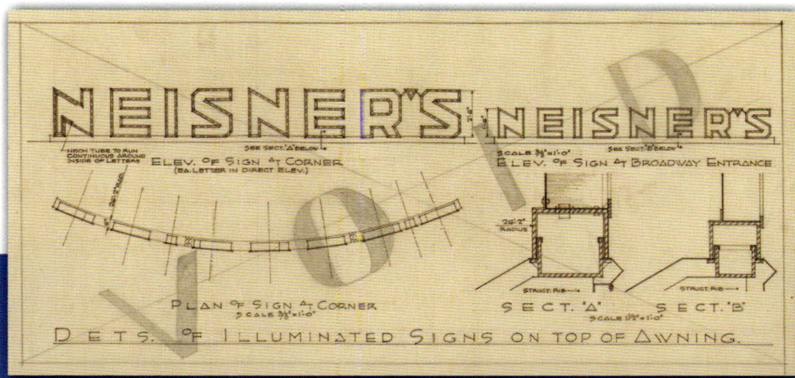

Signage detail, architectural drawing, Neisner's.

Casa de Mexico, located adjacent to the Alameda Theater (see page 72), housed the consulates of Mexico and several Latin American countries as well as the Mexican government's tourism office and a Mexican restaurant and curio shop when it opened. The signage shown in this architectural rendering was never installed.[30]

Mexican tile and colorful concealed lighting carry through from the exterior of the Casa de Mexico to its interior corridors.

Casa de Mexico International Building
318 West Houston Street, San Antonio
N. Straus Nayfach, architect
Victor Prassel Construction Co., contractor
1948

Entrance, Casa de Mexico.

Stair rail, Casa de Mexico.

Corridor, Casa de Mexico.

Terrazzo, Casa de Mexico.

Palomino Club Building
3401-3407 Guadalupe Street, Austin
ca. 1948

Storefronts, Palomino Club Building.

The glazed tile covering the exterior of the O.R. Mitchell Dodge dealership's "Million Dollar Showroom" was soft blue-green with yellow trim to prevent glare from distracting passing drivers. The building was demolished in November 2009.[31]

O.R. Mitchell Motors, demolished
1130 Broadway, San Antonio
Bartlett Cocke, architect
F.A. Nunnelly, contractor
1950

Texaco hired Walter Dorwin Teague, an architect and celebrated industrial designer, to create the prototype for its service stations. The company built the first of the new standard stations in 1938; the "Teague Texaco" remained the model for the company's stations until 1964.[32]

King's Texaco Service Station, later King's Service Station
1031 North St. Joseph Street, Gonzales
Walter Dorwin Teague (New York), architect
1951

KINGS
RUFUS KING
COOPERTIRES
DON'T GIVE UP A THING

Alameda Theater
318 West Houston Street, San Antonio
N. Straus Nayfach with Clarence Rinard,
Bernard McMahon and Russell White, architects
Victor Prassel Construction Co., contractor
1949

(Opposite)
Ticket booth, Alameda Theater, San Antonio.

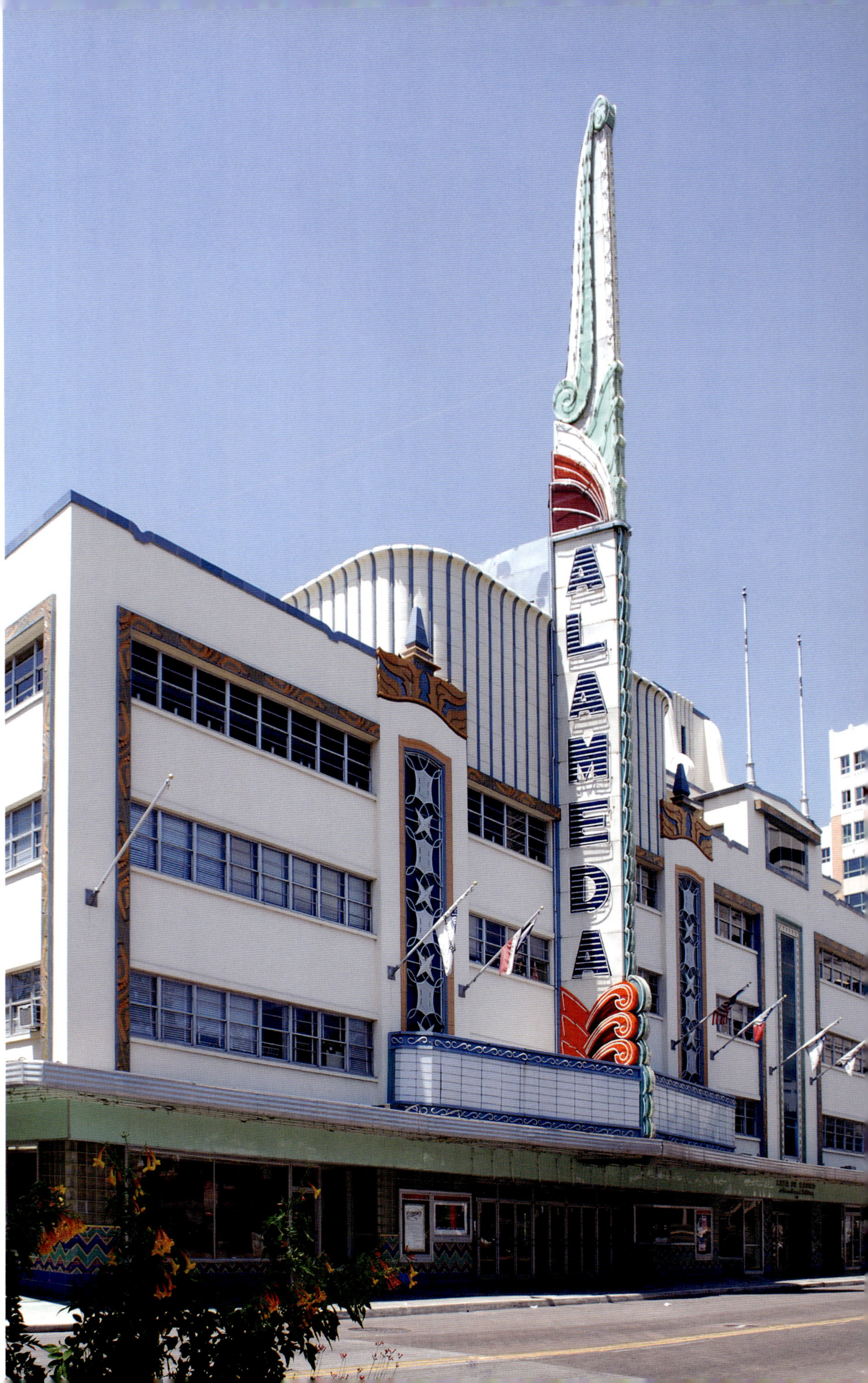

THEATERS

"The cathedral of Art, where the culture of two nations can converge."

La Prensa
March 9, 1949

By the late 1940s, the construction of elaborate downtown movie theaters was all but over in the United States. San Antonio had its share, all predating the Great Depression — but none was quite like the Alameda, one of the country's last great movie palaces.

At the time, the Alameda was the largest theater dedicated to Spanish-language entertainment ever built in the U. S., but developer G. A. Lucchese wanted it to be more than just a theater: He envisioned the Alameda and the adjacent Casa de Mexico (see page 66) as a lavish showplace for Mexican culture. To that end, architect N. Straus Nayfach and a team of interior designers filled the building with distinctive features. Colorful Mexican tiles drew patrons into the grand lobby, which featured artist Pedro Terán's aluminum sculptural set "Spirit of the Dance."[1]

Etched and backlit Plexiglas panels lined walls and staircases, and a series of

murals in the auditorium were executed in fluorescent paint that glowed under concealed black lights. Terán designed the murals, believed to be the largest of their kind still in existence, to depict the histories of Mexico and San Antonio, reinforcing the idea that the Alameda was a cultural meeting place. To drive the point home, lighthouses symbolizing the old and new worlds flanked the stage and were linked by a plaster ribbon that soared across the auditorium ceiling. Above it all, an 86-foot spire blazed with three-quarters of a mile of cold cathode tubing, a new landmark on the west side of downtown San Antonio.[2]

Nayfach found inspiration in the Teatro Chapultepec in Mexico City, which he visited while preparing plans for the Alameda. Architect S. Charles Lee gave the Chapultepec, which opened in 1944, sleek curved lines, mirrored walls, indirect lighting and a central sculptural group in the lobby — all of which became features of the Alameda's design as well. Sadly, Nayfach did not live to see his work completed; the architect died in 1948 when the theater was only half finished.[3]

The Alameda may have been the grandest modernistic theater built in the Hill Country, but it was far from the only one. Dozens of Deco theater construction and remodeling projects were completed in the 1930s and '40s, the result of Art Deco and Art Moderne's popularity coinciding with Hollywood's Golden Age. Prolific Dallas theater architects Jack Corgan and W. Scott Dunne designed many of the buildings, though even John Eberson of New York, best

Auditorium from balcony, Alameda Theater, shown 2009.

Auditorium rendering, Alameda Theater.

Auditorium from stage, Alameda Theater, shown 2009.

Flourescent mural, "History of San Antonio," Alameda Theater, Pedro Teràn, designer, Frank Lackner (Chicago), painter.

known for elaborate movie palaces like the San Antonio Majestic, also tried his hand at suburban Deco with San Antonio's Woodlawn Theater.

A surprising number of modernistic movie theaters survive in the Hill Country, particularly in San Antonio's inner suburbs and on small-town main streets. Some of them, like the Brauntex in New Braunfels, have been adapted for live performances, while others, like the Raye in Hondo, have operated as movie theaters since they were built.

(Top)
Grand foyer with "Sprit of the Dance," Alameda Theater, shown 1949.

(Bottom)
Auditorium, Alameda Theater, shown 1949.

Although the canopy's design is a mix of architectural styles, the Texas Theater building is Art Deco in its massing and detailing. This design foreshadows W. Scott Dunne's later modernistic work for the Interstate Amusement Co.

Texas Theater
425 North Austin Street, Seguin
W. Scott Dunne (Dallas), architect
1929

Decorative tile, Texas Theater.

Raye Theater
1707 Avenue M, Hondo
ca. 1932

Sign, Raye Theater.

Ticket booth, Raye Theater.

Dallas architect W. Scott Dunne was Texas' best known theater designer during the 1930s through his work for the Interstate, Jefferson, and Saenger theater chains.[4]

In 1935, professional journals reported Dunne was designing the remodeling of a theater in Taylor for the Taylor Amusement Company. Although the reports do not specify which of the company's theaters was being remodeled, historic photos strongly suggest that Dunne designed the updated Rita.[5]

The Rita Theater was renamed the Howard in 1950.

Rita Theater, later Howard Theater
308 North Main Street, Taylor
W. Scott Dunne (Dallas), architect, attributed
1935 (remodel)

Sign, Howard Theater.

Varsity Theater
2402 Guadalupe Street, Austin
W. Scott Dunne (Dallas), architect
1936

Varsity Theater, shown 1936.

(Opposite page clockwise from the top)
Palace Theater
810 South Austin Avenue, Georgetown
1938 (remodel)

Façade, Palace Theater.

State Theater
713 Congress Avenue, Austin
Central Contracting Co. (Dallas), contractor
1935

SHOWING

STATE

PALACE
PALACE
THE ODD COUPLE BY NEIL SIMON

BRAUNTEX
NBTC'S GUYS AND DOLLS JUN 13-28
BROADWAY'S BEST - A MUSICAL REVIEW
JUL 17&18 7:30PM JUL 19 2:30PM

As a young architect and licensed pilot, Jack Corgan built his practice flying to small cities and towns in Texas and surrounding states to design movie theaters.[6]

Brauntex Theater
209 West San Antonio Street, New Braunfels
Jack Corgan (Dallas), architect
1942

Sign detail, Brauntex Theater.

Ticket booth, Brauntex Theater.

John Eberson was one of the most prolific movie theater architects in the country. He is best remembered for designing the first atmospheric movie palaces in the 1920s.[7]

Woodlawn Theater
1920 Fredericksburg Road, San Antonio
John Eberson (New York), architect
1945

The Guadalupe served Mexican-American and Mexican neighborhoods on San Antonio's West Side. The theater's façade has been remodeled.

Guadalupe Theater, later Guadalupe Cultural Arts Center
1301 Guadalupe Street, San Antonio
N. Straus Nayfach, architect
1942

Palace Theater
314 South Austin Street, Seguin
1947

The relief panel over the Arcadia's entrance is the only visible remnant of the theater's original Spanish Colonial design. The Arcadia first opened in 1926.[8]

Arcadia Theater
717 Water Street, Kerrville
J.J. Fritch (Dallas), contractor
1948 (remodel)

Sign detail, Arcadia Theater.

Spanish colonial detail, Arcadia Theater.

Lynn Theater
510 St. Paul Street, Gonzales
Jack Corgan (Dallas), architect
L.A. Willard, contractor
1948

Signage detail, Lynn Theater.

Sign detail, Lynn Theater.

The Mission Drive-In is a rare surviving example of the Hill Country's outdoor theater architecture. In addition to the substantial screen tower, the drive-in's entrance originally sported a colorful mural of the historic Mission San José, which stands nearby. The Mission was San Antonio's last operating drive-in theater when it closed in 2007.

Mission Drive-In Theater, partially demolished
3100 Roosevelt Avenue, San Antonio
F.L. Scott & Son, contractor
1948

Stanley Theater
719 East Davis Street, Luling
Jack Corgan (Dallas), architect
1948

RESIDENTIAL

"It truly seems like a castle in the clouds that has come to earth."

Austin Building Magazine
August 1938

The image of the Bohn house descending from the clouds is not completely a flight of fancy. Owner Herbert Bohn reportedly found inspiration for his streamlined dream house in the luxury ocean liners of his day and the Academy Award-winning design of Shangri-La, the unlikely modernistic Tibetan lamasery from the 1937 motion picture Lost Horizon.[1]

Bohn was one of the owners of the successful Bohn Bros. department store, considered Austin's most innovative retailer. Bohn Bros. operated the city's first air-conditioned store and was the first to install plate glass windows; Herbert Bohn received national recognition for designing outstanding window displays. Bohn Bros. was also up-to-date in its architecture. A 1929 remodeling gave the Congress Avenue store a "moulded stone-and-grillwork front, the first example of that type of architecture on the avenue." The store's newspaper ad shows a building with a fairly modest modernistic façade.[2]

Residence for Mr. & Mrs. Herbert Bohn
1126 West Twenty-ninth Street, Austin
Roy L. Thomas, architect, with Herbert Bohn
Ernest W. Parker, contractor
1938

Solarium, Bohn house.

Although Herbert Bohn's influence on the store's design is not known, he was instrumental in creating his family's home. Bohn is credited with developing the design concept and detailed preliminary plans for the house. Architect Roy L. Thomas, a family friend, refined Bohn's original concept and produced the architectural drawings and specifications. Bohn's ultramodern ideas included a built-in radio speaker in the living room's acoustical tile ceiling, a tile goldfish pond in the solarium, and a curved sectional couch in the living room.[3]

The house's most distinctive feature, however, is the moon gate between the living and dining rooms. It is a motorized pocket door framed by a round portal and made of matched figured gum with a cherry finish, glass panels, and inlaid chromium strips. The family's three children dubbed this the "Magic Door" because it disappeared up into the wall at the flip of a switch.[4]

Neighborhood children had their own ideas about the building, which they dubbed "the ship house." Looking up from Shoal Creek at the basement portholes and curved solarium projecting from the hillside, it is easy to image the bow of a ship cutting through the waves. That may have been just what Bohn had in mind. He and his wife Alice sailed on an early voyage of the Queen Mary, a masterpiece of Art Deco design. Herbert Bohn also held an interest in the Bohn Travel Agency, listed in the 1937 Austin city directory under "Steam Ship Agents." The original plans for the house in the University of Texas' Alexander Architectural Archive include a brochure for the Queen Mary that Bohn apparently gave his architect.[5]

Modernistic houses were never common in Texas and almost nonexistent outside larger cities. San Antonio and Austin both have distinguished examples of modernistic homes and apartments, but the quality of Austin's residential design is surprising given the city's small size at the time. Austin's collection of modernistic homes is an indication of the state capital's growth during the Great Depression. Between 1930 and 1940, Austin's population rose by 39 percent, from 53,000 to almost 84,000.[6]

Bohn house.

Entrance, Bohn house.

"Moon gate", architectural drawing, Bohn house.

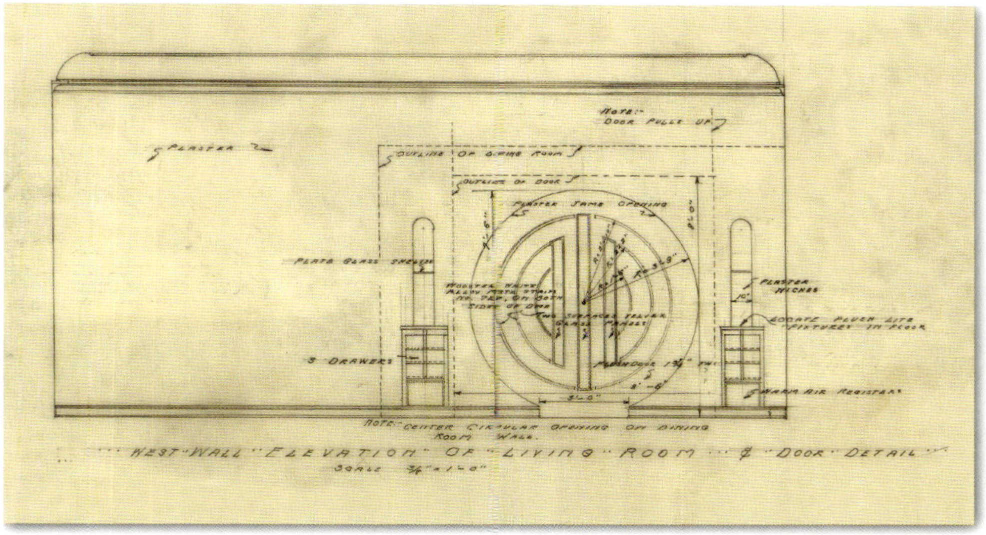

2201

The Berryhill residence was reportedly the first house in San Antonio built "in accordance with a strictly modern theory of design." In 1936, *Architectural Forum* magazine designated the house one of the outstanding small homes in the country.[7]

Residence for Mr. & Mrs. Dempsey Berryhill
2201 West Mulberry Avenue, San Antonio
Adams & Adams, architects
1935

Dining room, shown ca. 1935, Berryhill house.

Apartments
1509 West Woodlawn Avenue, San Antonio
1937

(Opposite)
Apartments
268 East Lullwood Avenue, San Antonio
N. Straus Nayfach, architect
D.B. Janssen, contractor
1938

268

A local society columnist described the apartment building at 337 East Lullwood Avenue as looking "very like a delectable wedding cake."[8]

Apartments
337 East Lullwood Avenue, San Antonio
Ellis Albaugh, architect
1938

Detail, 337 East Lullwood Avenue.

(Opposite)
Entry porch, 337 East Lullwood Avenue.

(Right)
Residence for Mr. & Mrs. E.D. "Ned" DePuy
330 East Summit Avenue, San Antonio
1938

Residence
325 King William Street, San Antonio
1940

Duplex for Dorothy Nichols
1206 Lorrain Street, Austin
1940

Duplex
1209 Elm Street, Austin
1948

Ellison-Photo
-Austin-

INSTITUTIONAL

"The best designs of public buildings that have been produced in the past 6 years indicate definite efforts to provide structures to fit our present civilization rather than to make our civilization fit into buildings that were designed for other ages."

Survey of the Architecture of Completed Projects of the Public Works Administration
May 1939

Modernistic institutional buildings generally fall into one of two categories: those built before the Great Depression and funded locally or those built during the Depression and funded with federal money. The former tended to be more elaborate, the latter more austere. In the Hill Country, one of the last major pre-Depression public buildings was the Travis County Courthouse in Austin, which opened in 1931, just as the region's economy began to decline.

Page Brothers' design for the courthouse was much more characteristic of the Jazz Age than anything that came later. Outside, strong vertical lines rose through a series of setbacks, exaggerating the building's height; exterior detailing was a somewhat unusual blend of Zigzag Deco and ancient Greek, including classically inspired reliefs above the principal entrances. Inside, courtrooms and corridors blended Egyptian details with the elaborate metalwork, cut stone, and inlaid wood typical of late 1920s Deco. Additions to the courthouse in 1958 and 1962, though sensitive, obscured some of the 1931 exterior architecture, and pressing space needs resulted in the alteration of many of the original interiors.[1]

As the Depression deepened, the Roosevelt administration funneled a then-unheard-of amount of money to public projects across the country in an attempt to stimulate the economy and provide jobs. Beginning in 1933, the Public Works Administration allocated more than $6 billion to more than 34,000 public projects, including roads, bridges, schools, government buildings, hospitals, and hydroelectric dams. Starting in 1936, the Works Progress Administration (later renamed the Work Projects Administration) pumped another $10.5 billion into similar projects. The architecture of these government-funded projects remained modernistic, but it was more stripped-down and restrained than what had come before. The Hill Country has some fine examples of this WPA Deco style, including Austin's 1936 United States Court House and 1939 Municipal Building.[2]

Travis County Courthouse
1000 Guadalupe Street, Austin
Page Brothers, architects
H.E. Wattinger, contractor
1931

Detail, Travis County Courthouse.

Murals painted under the direction of the Treasury Department's Section of Painting and Sculpture (later the Section of Fine Art) were an integral part of many federally funded projects in the 1930s, especially post offices. Well-preserved examples can be found throughout the Hill Country, most notably Howard Cook's *San Antonio's Importance in Texas History*, a fresco cycle in the lobby of San Antonio's 1937 central post office.[3]

Nearly every city and town in the area ended up with at least one PWA- or WPA-funded project. Post offices were the most common, especially in small towns, but few places enjoyed the government largesse experienced in Seguin, which had a population of 5,225 in 1930. Through the efforts of its

(Clockwise from left)
East entrance, Travis County Courthouse.

Lantern, Travis County Courthouse.

District courtroom, Travis County Courthouse, shown 1931.

Pedestal, Travis County Courthouse.

Detail, Travis County Courthouse.

well-connected mayor, Max Starcke, federal funds helped construct a new municipal building with library, public park with recreation building, swimming pool and nine-hole golf course, county courthouse and county jail as well as sidewalk and street repairs, sewer system upgrades, and hospital improvements.[4]

Although the San Antonio Municipal Auditorium exhibits Spanish and Moorish influences, the massing and abstraction of form in the ornamentation are modernistic. Ayres & Ayres' design for the administration building at Randolph Field (page 118) can be seen as a colossal version of one of the Municipal Auditorium's towers.

Municipal Auditorium
100 Auditorium Circle, San Antonio
Atlee B. & Robert M. Ayres with George R. Willis and Emmett T. Jackson, architects
Walsh & Burney Co., contractor
1926

Volute, Municipal Auditorium.

The San Antonio Club and the Casino Club merged in 1925 and constructed this joint facility two years later. The club building originally contained meeting and recreation rooms, banquet facilities, and overnight accommodations.[5]

The Meso-American detailing resulted from research the Kelwood Co. conducted at the National Museum in Mexico City and at Aztec, Zapotec, Toltec, and Mayan archeological sites. Designers used these findings to create San Antonio's Aztec Theater (1926) in addition to the San Antonio-Casino Club Building.[6]

(Clockwise from left)
San Antonio-Casino Club Building
102 West Crockett Street, San Antonio
Kelwood Co., architect
Heath & Kinsey, contractor
1927

Entrance, San Antonio-Casino Club Building.

Lintel, San Antonio-Casino Club Building.

Medallion, San Antonio-Casino Club Building.

CASINO CLUB
BUILDING

Until the end of segregation, this building served as an important educational facility and gathering place for San Antonio's African-American community. The auditorium was known for hosting performances by leading entertainers including Louis Armstrong, Ella Fitzgerald, Duke Ellington, and Count Basie.[7]

Colored Branch of the San Antonio Library and Auditorium, later Carver Community Cultural Center
215 North Hackberry Street, San Antonio
Seuter & Simons, architects
Mitchell Construction Co., contractor
1930

Side entrance, Colored Branch Library.

Detail, Colored Branch Library.

After the San Antonio Public Library moved to a new facility, this building housed the Hertzberg Circus Collection from 1968 to 2001.

San Antonio Public Library, later Hertzberg Circus Collection; Briscoe Museum of Western Art
210 Market Street, San Antonio
Herbert S. Green, architect
Kroeger-Brooks Construction Co., contractor
1930

Cervantes sculpture, San Antonio Public Library.

Shakespeare sculpture, San Antonio Public Library.

JOHN GREENLEAF
WHITTIER ACADEMY
2101

Thomas A. Edison High School, later John Greenleaf Whittier Junior High; Whittier Health Science Academy
2101 Edison Drive, San Antonio
Harvey P. Smith, architect
1930

Parapet detail, Edison High School.

"Service" relief, Edison High School.

When Randolph Field was built as the Air Corps Training Center, media referred to the new base as "The West Point of the Air." First Lieutenant Harold L. Clark developed the original concept for an "Air City" and was appointed supervising architect for the project. The Army commissioned several of San Antonio's leading architects to design specific facilities at Randolph; Ayres & Ayres won the contract for the base's centerpiece, Building 100.

Ayres & Ayres designed the administration building with Spanish and Moorish influences, giving it a 170-foot tower that conceals a 500,000-gallon water tank. Flyers have called Building 100 the "Taj Mahal" from its earliest days. Randolph Field Historic District is listed on the National Register of Historic Places.[8]

Building 100, "Taj Mahal"
Randolph Field, later Randolph Air Force Base, San Antonio
Atlee B. & Robert M. Ayers, architects
1931

Tower, "Taj Mahal."

In 1942, artist William Dean Fausett received a Guggenheim Foundation fellowship to create a 1,272-square-foot mural for the cadet mess hall at Randolph Field. Fausett painted 6-foot by 24-foot panels depicting six scenes in the training lives of pilots, navigators, and bombardiers. He completed the mural in 1944.[9]

Around 1950, the artwork was sent to the U. S. Air Force Academy. Only one section, "His First Solo Flight," survives; it hangs in the Parachute Room at the academy in Colorado Springs. Fausett's studies for the mural remain at Randolph Air Force Base where they are displayed in the Air Education and Training Command building.

After he completed the mural project, Fausett received a second Guggenheim fellowship to create four life-sized portraits of a pilot, navigator, bombardier, and gunner for the rotunda of Randolph's administration building. Fausett used the top floor of Building 100 as his studio when he was painting the 4-foot by 6-foot oil portraits. In 2009, the Air Force Art Program Office funded the restoration of the four Fausett paintings, which continue to hang in Building 100.[10]

Pages 120 and 121
(Bottom left and right)
"His First Solo Flight," study for mural
William Dean Fausett, artist.

"Navigators Studying the Stars," study for mural.

(Top left to right) Pilot portrait, Building 100.

Navigator portrait, Building 100.

Bombardier portrait, Building 100.

Gunner portrait, Building 100.

160

(Clockwise from left)

Central Catholic High School

1403 North St. Mary's Street, San Antonio
Henry Dreisoener (St. Louis), architect
McKenzie Construction Co., contractor
1932

Cross, Central Catholic High School.

Entrance, Central Catholic High School.

Pilaster detail, Central Catholic High School.

CENTRAL CATHOLIC
HIGH SCHOOL
1403

With a construction budget of $1.25 million, Thomas Jefferson High School was the most expensive public school built in the United States up to that time. After a United Press survey deemed Jefferson the country's best high school, *Life* magazine featured the school in a March 1938 cover story. The next month, Fox Movietone News released a newsreel filmed at "America's most modern school." [11]

Father and son craftsmen Hannibal and Eugene Pianta modeled and cast the art stone ornamentation for Jefferson High School.[12]

Thomas Jefferson High School
723 Donaldson Avenue, San Antonio
Adams & Adams, architects
Walsh, Burney & Key, contractor
1932

Detail, Thomas Jefferson High School.

South wing, Thomas Jefferson High School.

Detail, Thomas Jefferson High School.

Molding detail, Thomas Jefferson High School.

DO NOT
ENTER

(Clockwise from left)

State Highway Building, later Dewitt C. Greer State Highway Building
125 East Eleventh Street, Austin
Adams & Adams with Lang & Witchell (Dallas), architects
J.E. Morgan & Sons (El Paso), contractor
1933

Entrance, State Highway Building.

Detail, State Highway Building.

Capital, State Highway Building.

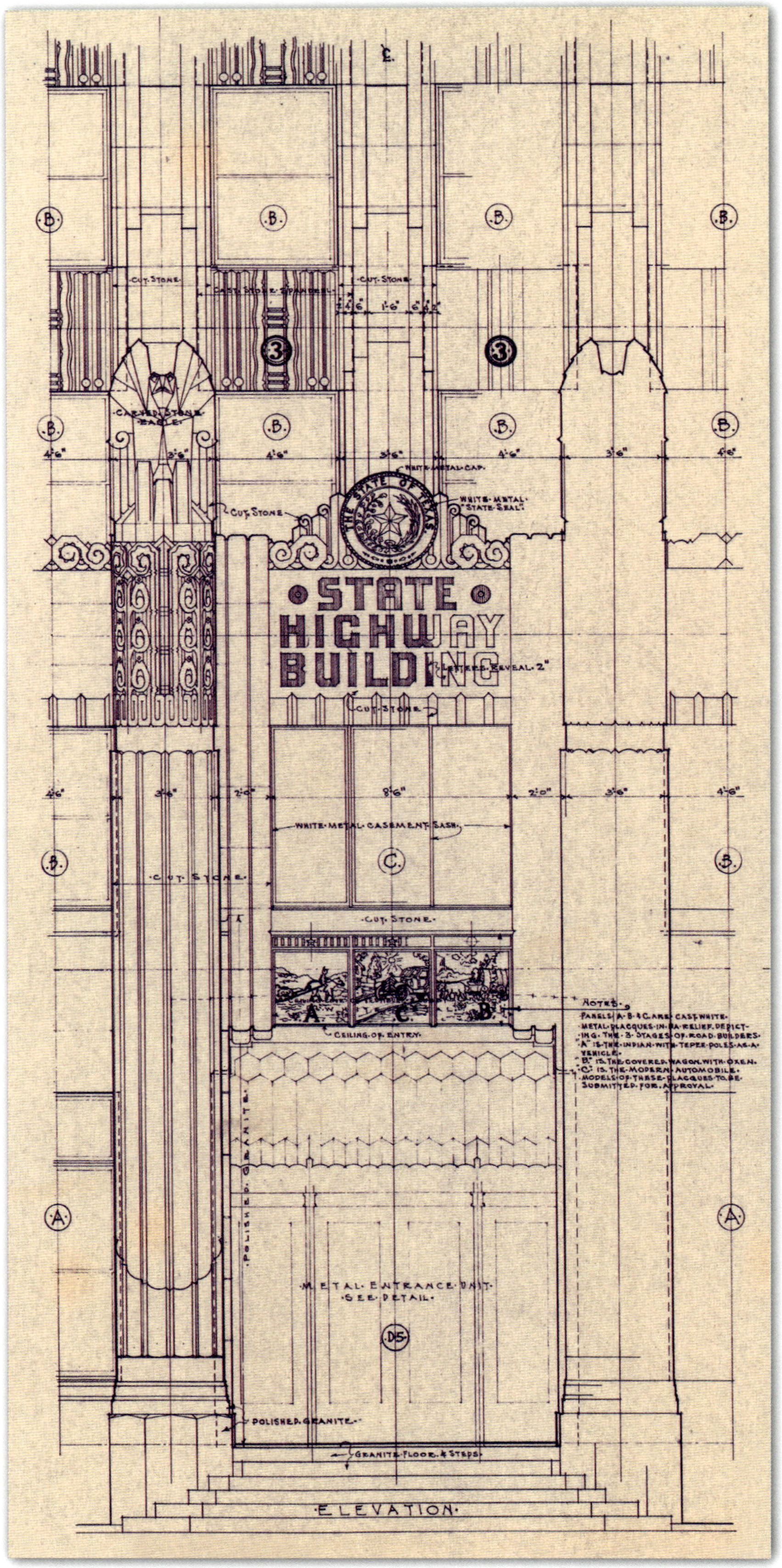

Entrance blueprint, State Highway Building.

Entrance detail, State Highway Building.

Vents in the lobby of the State Highway Building are covered by unusual marble grilles carved with the shapes of road rollers.

The building's hearing room retains many of its original architectural details, including streamlined brackets (left) bearing Texas lone stars.

(Clockwise from left)
Lobby details, State Highway Building.

Detail, hearing room, State Highway Building

Seguin Municipal Building
205 North River Street, Seguin
L.M. Wirtz (Houston), architect
1935

Relief, Seguin Municipal Building.

Taylor City Hall
400 North Main Street, Taylor
E.H. Leinbach (Dallas), architect
Frank Sefcik, contractor
1935

Stinson Field Administration Building, later Stinson Municipal Airport
8535 Mission Road, San Antonio
Henry T. Phelps, architect
1936

Entrance, Stinson Field Administration Building.

Guadalupe County Courthouse
101 East Court Street, Seguin
Wirtz & Calhoun (Houston), architects
Vincent Falbo & Sons, contractor
1936

"Justice" relief, Guadalupe County Courthouse.

"Wisdom" relief, Guadalupe County Courthouse.

Taylor High School Gymnasium
400 block West Ninth Street, Taylor
Hugo F. Kuehne, architect
E.B. Snead, contractor
1936

Entrance, Taylor High School Gymnasium.

Detail, Taylor High School Gymnasium.

Becker Elementary School
906 West Milton Street, Austin
Giesecke & Harris, architects
1936

Blackshear Elementary School
1712 East Eleventh Street, Austin
Giesecke & Harris, architects
Rex D. Kitchens, contractor
1936

United States Court House
200 West Eighth Street, Austin
Louis A. Simon (Washington, D. C.), supervising architect
C.H. Page & Son with Kenneth Franzheim (New York), architects
Algernon Blair (Montgomery, Alabama), contractor
1936

Details, U.S. Court House.

(Clockwise from left)
Courtroom, U.S. Court House, Austin.

Metalwork, U.S. Court House.

Courtroom entrance, U.S. Court House.

Door, U.S. Court House.

HORACE MANN
JUNIOR HIGH SCHOOL

Horace Mann Junior High School,
later Young Women's Leadership Academy
2123 West Huisache Avenue, San Antonio
Atlee B. & Robert M. Ayres, architects
King B. Key, contractor
1937

(This page: clockwise from right)
Entrance detail, Horace Mann Junior High School.

Masonry grille, Horace Mann Junior High School.

Detail, Horace Mann Junior High School.

UNION STATE BANK
600
TEAM USB
WE PLAY FOR YOU!!!
Union State Bank
830-792-6655
600 MAIN

Kerrville City Hall, later Union State Bank
600 Main Street, Kerrville
Phelps & Dewees, architects
1937

Lantern, Kerrville City Hall.

Lampasas Junior High School
207 East Avenue A, Lampasas
1938

Austin Municipal Building
124 West Eighth Street, Austin
Page & Southerland, architects
Schwarzer-Barron Co., contractor
1938 (remodel)

Entrance, Austin Municipal Building.

Light fixtures, Austin Municipal Building.

Sconce, Austin Municipal Building.

Central Fire Station No. 1
Fifth and Trinity streets, Austin
Kreisle & Brooks, architects
Yarbrough Construction Co., contractor
1938

German immigrants founded the Sons of Hermann as a mutual aid society in New York in 1840. The first lodge in Texas was formed in San Antonio in 1860; Texas' Grand Lodge was established in San Antonio in 1890.[13]

Hermann Sons Grand Lodge
515 South St. Mary's Street, San Antonio
Leo M.J. Dielmann, architect
Guido Brothers Construction Co., contractor
1938

PARKS & RECREATION

Robert H. H. Hugman created the original designs for San Antonio's River Walk.[14]

Seguin Recreation Building
Max Starcke Park, Seguin
Robert H.H. Hugman, architect
1938

Stairway to rooftop terrace, Seguin Recreation Building.

Detail, Seguin Recreation Building.

UNITED STATES POST OFFICE
GIDDINGS TEXAS
78942
PASSPORT
U.S. Pa
Photos
UNITED STATES POSTAL SERVICE

Government architects with the Treasury Department's Office of the Supervising Architect created a series of standard designs for small-town post offices in different regions of the country. Post Office officials selected the design that would be built in a given community with input from the local postmaster. Louis A. Simon, whose name appears on the cornerstones of virtually every Depression-era post office in Texas, was Supervising Architect from 1933 to 1939.[15]

Federal law set aside 1 percent of the total construction cost of post offices for "embellishment," which included paying the salaries of mural artists.[16]

U.S. Post Office
79 East Austin Street, Giddings
Louis A. Simon (Washington, D. C.), supervising architect
1938

Mural, "Cowboys Receiving the Mail"
U.S. Post Office, Giddings
Otis Dozier, artist
1939

Mural detail, "Cowboys Receiving the Mail."

UNITED STATES POST OFFICE
SMITHVILLE TEXAS
78957

U. S. Post Office
400 Main Street, Smithville
Louis A. Simon (Washington, D. C.), supervising architect
1938

Mural detail, "The Law - Texas Rangers"
U.S. Post Office, Smithville
Minnette Teichmueller, artist
1939

Mural detail, "The Law - Texas Rangers."

U. S. Post Office, later Kerr Arts & Cultural Center
228 Earl Garrett Street, Kerrville
Louis A. Simon (Washington, D. C.), supervising architect
Atlee B. & Robert M. Ayres, architects
Templeton-Cannon Co. (San Angelo), contractor
1936

Window grille, U.S. Post Office.

Roberson Hall was the residence hall for the former Medical and Surgical Memorial Hospital School of Nursing.[17]

(Opposite)
Martha Roberson Hall
509 Richmond Avenue, San Antonio
Phelps & Dewees & Simmons, architects
1939

NO PARKING
PASSENGER
LOADING
15

U. S. Post Office
21 North Avenue C., Elgin
Louis A. Simon (Washington, D. C.), supervising architect
1939

Grille, U.S. Post Office.

Mural detail, "Texas Farm"
U.S. Post Office, Elgin
Julius Woeltz, artist
1940

Mural detail, "Texas Farm."

Mural detail, "The Pony Express Station"
U.S. Post Office
217 West Market Street, Lockhart
John Law Walker, artist
1939

Mural detail, "The Pony Express Station."

Howard Cook, a New Mexico artist, won a Guggenheim Fellowship in 1932 to study fresco techniques in Mexico. There he encountered the work of Diego Rivera, whose style influenced Cook's 16-panel fresco cycle *San Antonio's Importance in Texas History*. The murals, one of the largest true fresco groups in the United States, were restored in 1999.[18]

Cook used San Antonio residents as models for the figures in the murals.[19]

Fresco detail, "Cattle Trail,"
San Antonio's Importance in Texas History
U.S. Post Office
615 East Houston Street, San Antonio
Howard Cook, artist
1939

Fresco detail, "Houston Presents Sword at First Congress of Texas Republic,"
San Antonio's Importance in Texas History.

Fresco detail, "Torch-light Parade,"
San Antonio's Importance in Texas History.

(Opposite)
Fresco detail, "Last Stand at the Alamo,"
San Antonio's Importance in Texas History.

Robert E. Lee Elementary School
3308 Hampton Road, Austin
Roy L. Thomas, architect
1939

Signage, Robert E. Lee Elementary School.

Gillespie County Courthouse
101 West Main Street, Fredericksburg
Edward Stein, architect
Hill & Combs, contractors
1939

Signage, Gillespie County Courthouse.

The federal Work Projects Administration constructed Alamo Stadium along the contours of a former limestone quarry. Affectionately dubbed "the Big Rock Pile," it is Texas' largest high school football stadium, seating 23,000.[20]

The Work Projects Administration's arts and crafts program produced *100 Years of Sports in San Antonio, Texas, 1840-1940*, a series of four original tile murals installed over the main entrance of Alamo Stadium. The WPA trained workers to create the tiles using traditional Mexican techniques.[21]

Alamo Stadium
110 Tuleta Drive, San Antonio
Phelps & Dewees & Simmons, architects
1940

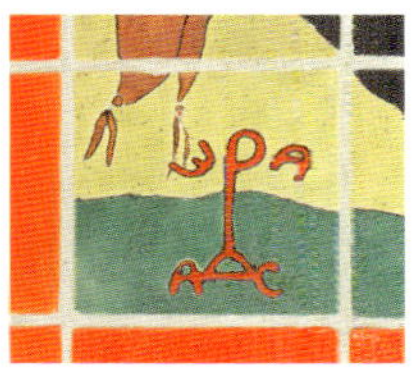

(Clockwise from left)
Ticket booth, Alamo Stadium.

"La Pelea del Gallo/El Jarabe Tapatio (The Cock Fight/Hat Dance Contest)," *100 Years of Sports in San Antonio, Texas, 1840-1940*
Alamo Stadium, San Antonio
Ethel Wilson Harris, designer
1941

"High School Sports," *100 Years of Sports in San Antonio, Texas, 1840-1940*, Alamo Stadium.

Craftmark, Work Projects Administration Arts and Crafts, Alamo Stadium.

Sixty members of the National Youth Administration, a New Deal agency under the Works Progress Administration, constructed the Vocational Agriculture Building (right) at Gonzales High School.[22]

Gonzales Auditorium, Gymnasium and High School Building
902 St. Louis Street, Gonzales
John M. Marriott, architect
1941

Vocational Agriculture Building
942 St. Louis Street, Gonzales
1940

First Evangelical Lutheran Church, later First Lutheran Church
1206 St. Joseph Street, Gonzales
Rudolph Nagel, architect
Sanctuary, 1942
Bell tower and annex, 1952

Bell tower, First Evangelical Lutheran Church.

The Works Progress Administration constructed the first phase of San Antonio's famous River Walk between 1939 and 1941. WPA Arts and Crafts produced the murals installed along the downtown riverfront.

River Walk
North bank at Navarro Street bridge, San Antonio
Tile mural, "Old Mill Crossing"
Ethel Wilson Harris, designer
1942

"Twin Cypress", North bank at North River Loop Gate, River Walk.
1942

Federal funding for the remodeling and expansion of the 1928 State Hygienic Laboratory was secured weeks before the attack on Pearl Harbor, making the State Health Building one of the few non-military construction projects carried out after the United States entered World War II. The Health Department added the fourth floor in 1948; the porthole windows and tower were installed during the building's conversion to residential use in 1999.[23]

State Health Building, later Anson Jones State Office Building; Avenue Lofts
410 East Fifth Street, Austin
John Linn Scott, architect
1943

Bexar County Coliseum,
later Joe & Harry Freeman Coliseum
3201 East Houston Street, San Antonio
Bartlett Cocke with Atlee B. & Robet M. Ayres and
Phelps & Dewees & Simmons, architects
Walsh & Burney Co., contractor
1949

Memorial Fire & Police Station,
later Seguin Central Fire Station
110 Elm Street, Seguin
Marvin Eickenroht, architect
B.J. Smith, contractor
1949

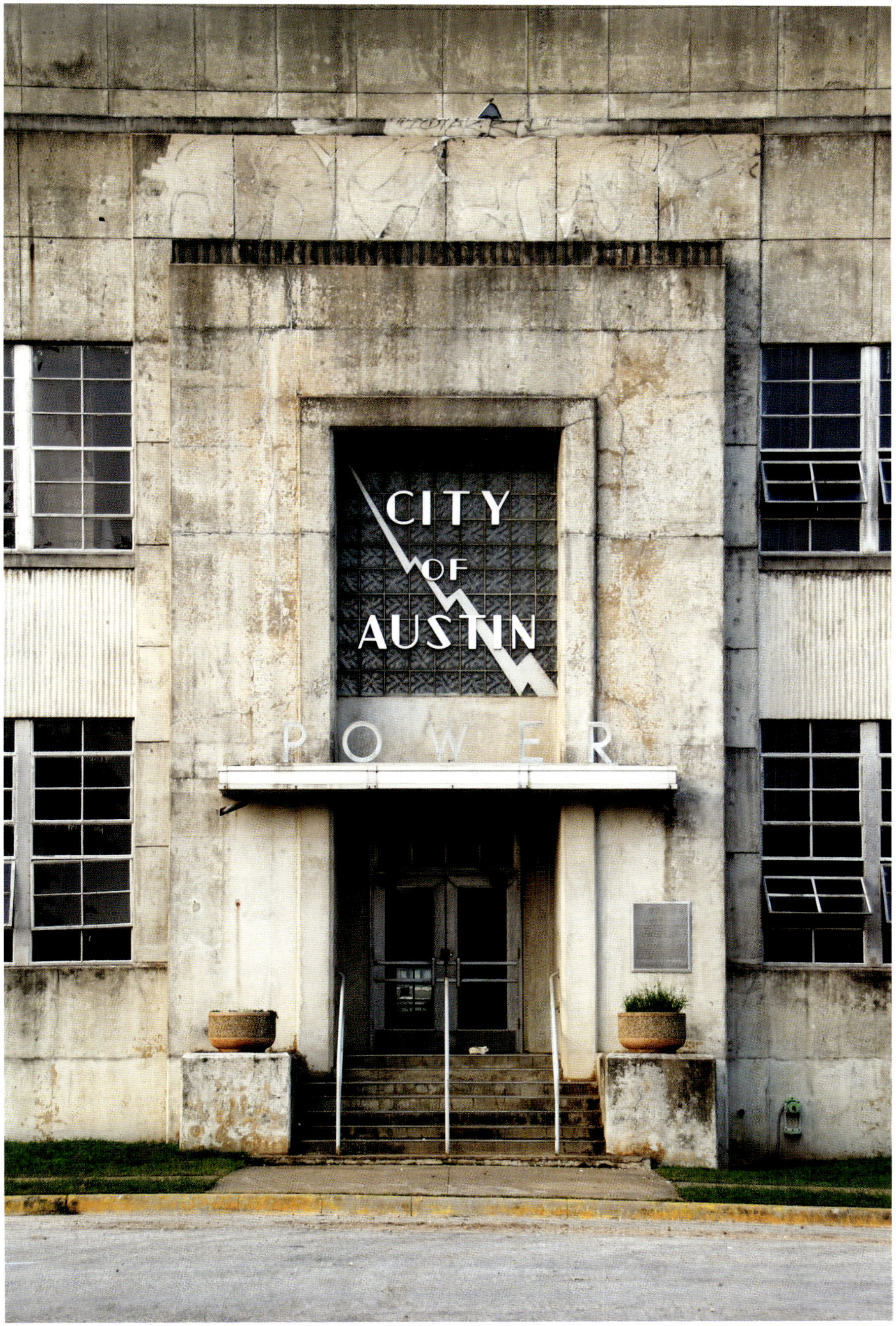

In 1960, Austin City Council named the plant for Walter E. Seahclm, superintendent of Austin's water and power department from 1922 to 1955.[24]

Power Plant No. 2, later Seaholm Power Plant
800 West Cesar Chavez Street, Austin
Burns & McDonnell (Kansas City), engineers/architects
J.M. Odom Construction Co., contractor
1950

Sign, Power Plant No. 2.

Henry J. Steinbomer, who specialized in ecclesiastical architecture, designed the Youth Building as part of an ambitious project that would have replaced all of Travis Park Methodist Church's historic structures. To save money, the congregation chose to remodel the existing Harmony Hall (ca. 1895) and install a new façade; the rest of the project was never built.

The building's stained glass projects above the roofline, and at certain times of day the sun illuminates the figure of Christ as seen at left.[25]

Travis Park Methodist Youth Building
613 Navarro Street, San Antonio
Henry J. Steinbomer, architect
Howard Bumbaugh, contractor
1950 (remodel)

Relief, Travis Park Methodist Youth Building.

St. Austin's Catholic Church and Rectory
2026 Guadalupe Street, Austin
Walter Cocke, Jr. & Company (Waco), architects
J.M. Odom Construction Co., contractor
1953

Sconce, St. Austin's Catholic Church.

ERECTED TO COMMEMORATE THE HEROIC PERIOD OF EARLY TEXAS HISTORY AND TO
CELEBRATE A CENTURY OF THE INDEPENDENCE AND PROGRESS OF TEXAS AS A REPUBLIC AND STATE
AND DEDICATED TO THE STUDY OF THE NATURAL SCIENCES AND CIVIC HISTORY
TEXAS

COMMEMORATIVE

"*The preservers of history are as heroic as its makers.*"

Pat M. Neff, governor of Texas 1921-25, advocating for a Texas centennial celebration

Although Fair Park in Dallas was the centerpiece of the 1936 celebrations of the centennial of the Texas Revolution, commemorative buildings and monuments were constructed across the state during the last half of the 1930s under the auspices of the Commission for Control of Texas Centennial Celebrations. Among them was the Texas Memorial Museum on the campus of the University of Texas at Austin. The museum was partially funded by the sale of specially minted half-dollar coins designed by sculptor Pompeo Coppini, who also executed the sculpture on another centennial project, the Alamo Cenotaph.[1]

Houston architect John F. Staub designed the museum with a large central block flanked by low wings, but when work began on the building in 1936, funding was only available for the central portion and the wings were never constructed. Even so, the museum as built — with massive fluted piers framing three windows overlooking the UT campus — is typical of the "modern classicism" of Paul Philippe Cret of Philadelphia, who created a master plan for the university in 1933 and served as consulting architect on 19 campus buildings, including the museum. When it opened in 1939, the Texas Memorial Museum held a variety of items collected during the centennial, including documents and artifacts from the UT archives, antique china and crystal, and a series of dioramas donated by Humble Oil.[2]

Other centennial projects in the Hill Country varied in style. In Gonzales, San Antonio architecture firm Phelps & Dewees designed an Egyptian-influenced museum and amphitheater complex to commemorate the town's role in the Texas Revolution, and in La Grange, Page & Southerland of Austin marked the tomb of the victims of the Dawson Massacre and the Mier Expedition with a 48-foot monument featuring a cameo mural by artist Pierre Bourdelle. One of the last centennial monuments erected was the Alamo Cenotaph in San Antonio, a shaft of gray Georgia marble ringed by Coppini's portrait sculptures of Alamo defenders. Though the monument itself has modernistic lines, Coppini's work is fairly traditional — hardly surprising for a sculptor who referred to more abstract work as "modern debauchery of art."[3]

Texas Memorial Museum
2400 Trinity Street, Austin
John F. Staub (Houston) with Paul P. Cret (Philadelphia), architects
J.E. Morgan & Sons (El Paso), contractor
1939

"Texas Natural Resources," relief, Texas Memorial Museum, William Mozart McVey, sculptor

(*Clockwise from top left*)
West façade, Texas Memorial Museum, shown 1939.

East entrance, Texas Memorial Museum.

Corner detail, Texas Memorial Museum.

"Pioneer Man and Woman" relief, Texas Memorial Museum, William Mozart McVey, sculptor.

TEXAS
MEMORIAL MUSEUM
US
1937

The memorial on Monument Hill in La Grange honors men who died in two separate incidents. In 1842, an invading Mexican army killed 32 members of Nicholas Dawson's small Texas militia company after Dawson raised a flag of surrender. Later that year, a larger Texan force set out to avenge the Dawson Massacre. The Mexican army captured many of the soldiers and forced the prisoners to participate in the infamous Black Bean Lottery in which those who drew white beans lived and those who drew black beans were executed. During the Mexican-American War, the remains of those killed in the black bean incident and the Dawson Massacre were exhumed and reinterred on Monument Hill.[4]

The monument was dedicated in 1936 and features a cameo mural commemorating the Black Bean Lottery. French artist Pierre Bourdelle included three handprints in his design of the mural on the pylon. Bourdelle scratched his name into the center handprint; the names of his assistants are on the flanking handprints.

Mier Expedition and Dawson's Men Memorial
Monument Hill and Kreische Brewery State Park
414 State Loop 92, La Grange
Page & Southerland, architects
L.W. Stolz, contractor
1936

Cameo mural, Monument Hill, Pierre Bourdelle, artist.

Angel, Monument Hill, Raoul Josset, sculptor.

Bourdelle handprint, Monument Hill.

The Gonzales Memorial Museum commemorates the town's role in the Texas War for Independence. In 1835, eighteen men from Gonzales refused to surrender the town's cannon to the Mexican army and fired the first shots of what became the Texas Revolution. The building is a modernistic interpretation of an Egyptian mortuary temple.[5]

French sculptor Raoul Josset created the monument at the head of the museum's reflecting pool. The bronze figure honors the "Immortal 32," men and boys from Gonzales who answered William Barrett Travis' call for support and died with Travis defending the Alamo.

A memorial tablet located between the museum and amphitheater honors the "Old 18," men from Gonzales who fired the first shots in Texas' War for Independence.

(Opposite)

Gonzales Memorial Museum and Amphitheater
414 Smith Street, Gonzales
Phelps & Dewees, architects
Walsh & Burney Co., contractor
1937

Egyptian inspired detail, Gonzales Memorial Museum.

(This page, clockwise from left)
Gonzales Memorial Amphitheater.

Defenders of the Alamo Memorial
Gonzales Memorial Museum
Page & Southerland, architects
Raoul Josset, sculptor
1937

Light fixture, Gonzales Memorial Museum.

"Old 18" Memorial, Gonzales Memorial Museum.

The Alamo Cenotaph serves as a symbolic grave marker for the Alamo defenders. Cenotaph is Greek for "empty tomb"; no bodies are buried here. The monument was dedicated on Armistice Day, November 11, 1940.[6]

Sculptor Pompeo Coppini created the main figure on the pylon, "Spirit of the Alamo," which rises from the bodies of slain Alamo defenders. The sides of the monument feature more of Coppini's work: heroic statues of four heroes of the Alamo. James B. Bonham and Jim Bowie are depicted on the east side of the cenotaph, William Barrett Travis and Davy Crockett on the west.[7]

Alamo Cenotaph
Alamo Plaza, San Antonio
Adams & Adams, architects
Guido Brothers Construction Co., contractor
Rodriguez Brothers Monument Co., installation
1940

"Spirit of Sacrifice", Alamo Cenotaph
Pompeo Coppini, sculptor.

Portrait sculptures of Jim Bowie and James B. Bonham, Alamo Cenotaph.

ARCHITECTS AND ARTISTS

ADAMS & ADAMS was a well-respected San Antonio architecture firm. Carl C. Adams (1881-1918) and his nephew Carleton W. Adams (1885-1964) established their partnership in 1909, when Carleton graduated from Columbia University. After Carl Adams' death, Max C. Frederick joined the firm, although it kept the name Adams & Adams. As associate architect, Frederick played a key role in designing the company's modernistic projects, including the landmark Thomas Jefferson High School and the streamlined Berryhill residence.[1]

JOSÉ ARPA (1858-1952), painter, was born in Carmona, Spain and received his formal training at the Escuela de Belles Artes in Seville. He won the prestigious Prix de Rome in 1884, 1885, and 1886. Arpa moved to Mexico in 1895 when the government invited him to teach at the National Academy of Fine Arts; four years later, the painter traveled to San Antonio to participate in the International Fair of Art. He eventually settled in San Antonio and opened the Arpa School of Painting. After the installation of his murals in the San Antonio Express News Building in 1930, Arpa returned to Spain and remained there until his death.[2]

ATLEE B. & ROBERT M. AYRES was San Antonio's most prominent architecture firm from the 1920s through the 1940s. This father and son partnership designed some of the city's most significant buildings. Atlee Bernard Ayres (1873-1969) received his formal architectural training at New York's Metropolitan Museum of Art under the supervision of Columbia University. He first established his practice in San Antonio in 1894. His son Robert Moss Ayres (1898-1977) joined the firm around 1922 after graduating from the University of Pennsylvania School of Architecture and working in the New York offices of McKim, Mead & White.[3]

PIERRE BOURDELLE (1903-1966), sculptor and muralist, and **RAOUL JOSSET** (1899-1957), sculptor, were French-born artists whose careers took them to Texas during the Great Depression. Bourdelle's father, Émile-Antoine Bourdelle, was assistant to the sculptor August Rodin and a successful artist in his own right. The elder Bourdelle trained his son and Josset among many other students. Organizers of the 1936 Texas Centennial Exposition hired the artists individually to create works for what is now Fair Park in Dallas. After the exposition, the men collaborated on the centennial project for Monument Hill in La Grange. Josset settled in Texas and produced several other significant works for the state's centennial, including memorials at Gonzales and Goliad. Bourdelle continued his art career at the 1939 New York World's Fair.[4]

BARTLETT COCKE (1901-1992), architect, graduated from the University of Texas in 1922 before enrolling in the School of Architecture at the Massachusetts Institute of Technology. He apprenticed as a draftsman at the Kelwood Co. in San Antonio before establishing his own practice. During the Great Depression, Cocke created detailed measured drawings of antebellum buildings in Texas for the Historic American Buildings Survey. His residential designs, inspired by the historic houses he had documented, attracted the attention of national magazines. He received his first major commission in 1938, designing the iconic façade of Joske's department store on Alamo Plaza in San Antonio.[5]

POMPEO COPPINI (1870-1957), sculptor, grew up in Florence, Italy where he studied at l'Accademia di Belle Arti. He immigrated to the United States in 1896 and moved to Texas five years later when he won the commission to create the figures for the Confederate memorial on the State Capitol grounds. Coppini completed 36 public monuments during his career; among the best known are the Littlefield Fountain on the campus of the University of Texas at Austin and the Alamo Cenotaph in San Antonio. He later headed the art department at Trinity University in San Antonio and founded the Coppini Academy of Fine Arts.[6]

GIESECKE & HARRIS was a prominent Austin-based architecture firm that operated from 1921 to 1941. Bertram E. Giesecke (1892-1950) and A. Watkins "Watt" Harris (1893-1968) met as students at the University of Texas where they studied under Hugo F. Kuehne. In 1913, Giesecke earned the university's first architecture degree. The partners designed commercial and public buildings throughout the state and had a strong reputation for school design. Their most significant modernistic creation is the Merchants & Manufacturers Building (1930) in Houston, now the University of Houston–Downtown.[7]

HERBERT S. GREEN (1874-1957), architect, trained in the offices of William, Wallace & Flockhart in his native London. Around 1900, Green accepted a job with Alfred Giles, an English architect who had established a successful practice in Texas and Mexico. Green served as chief draftsman at Giles' branch office in Monterrey before transferring to the San Antonio office. Green established his own firm after Giles' death in 1920.[8]

ETHEL WILSON HARRIS (1893-1984), artist, moved with her family at a young age from Sabinal, Texas, to San Antonio, where she became interested in Mexican handicrafts. In 1931 she organized a workshop, Mexican Arts and Crafts, to promote traditional crafts such as basket weaving, pottery making, metalwork, and tilework. Harris' art tile designs became well known. Her tiles were sold nationwide and displayed at the 1933 and 1939 world's fairs, the 1936 Texas Centennial Exposition and HemisFair in 1968. Harris eventually ran three tile factories, collectively known as the San José Workshops. In 1939, she was named technical supervisor over arts and crafts projects of the Works Progress Administration in San Antonio; under her guidance, tile murals were installed in several locations around the city, including Randolph Air Force Base, the River Walk, and the San Antonio Zoo. Harris was one of the founders of the San Antonio Conservation Society and was especially interested in preserving the city's missions. She moved to the grounds of Mission San José in 1939 and lived there for more than 40 years, serving as the mission's first site manager.[9]

KELWOOD CO. was a development firm that began building houses in San Antonio's Monte Vista subdivision in 1924 and soon moved on to larger commercial projects. Robert B. Kelly (1892-1932), vice president and company architect, was the "Kel" in Kelwood. The firm is best known for the distinctive Aztec Theater and San Antonio-Casino Club Building, both designed in exotic Meso-American style.[10]

KREISLE & BROOKS was an Austin architecture firm that designed several important public buildings along with many houses and stores. Edwin C. Kreisle (1888-1971), an Austin native, attended the University of Texas and the Bradley Polytechnic Institute in Peoria, Illinois. R. Max Brooks (1907-1982) earned a bachelor's degree from the University of Texas and a master's degree from the Massachusetts Institute of Technology. In 1937, Kreisle & Brooks were co-architects with Giesecke & Harris and Page & Southerland on Federal Housing Project No. 1, the first public housing authorized by Congress. Brooks was later one of the co-architects of the Manned Spacecraft Center (later Lyndon B. Johnson Space Center) in Houston and the Lyndon Baines Johnson Library and Museum in Austin.[11]

HUGO F. KUEHNE (1884-1963), architect, graduated from the University of Texas School of Engineering in 1906 before earning a degree in architecture from the Massachusetts Institute of Technology. In 1910, Kuehne was practicing in Boston when the University of Texas hired him to head its newly established School of Architecture and serve as its first faculty member. He established a successful private practice in Austin in 1915 and continued working for almost five decades.[12]

N. STRAUS NAYFACH (1906 or 1907-1948), architect, earned his degree in architectural engineering from the University of Texas in 1928. On completing college, Nayfach volunteered to work free for the contractor constructing the Alamo National Building in San Antonio; after three months Nayfach was promoted to supervising architect on the project and kept his office in the building throughout his career. Nayfach strongly believed that middle class homeowners deserved good architectural design; much of his work consists of relatively small houses and apartment buildings. Although his given name was Nathaniel, in the late 1930s Nayfach changed his name to N. Straus Nayfach after meeting Nathan Straus, an early advocate for public housing.[13]

CHARLES HENRY PAGE (1876-1957), architect, moved with his family from St. Louis to Austin where his father, a mason and contractor, worked on the construction of the Texas State Capitol. The younger Page attended Austin public schools and trained in the office of architect Burt McDonald. C. H. Page set up his own practice in 1895 and designed the Texas Building for the 1904 Louisiana Purchase Exposition in St. Louis. His brother Louis C. Page (died 1934) later joined the firm, which was renamed C. H. PAGE & BROTHER (later PAGE BROTHERS). The partners went on to design many Texas county courthouses. In 1936, the firm was again renamed, this time as C. H. PAGE & SON, after C. H. Page, Jr. (1910-1988) earned his architecture degree from the University of Texas. C. H. Page, Jr. maintained the practice for more than 40 years.[14]

PAGE & SOUTHERLAND was the partnership of Louis C. Page, Jr. (1909-1981) and Louis F. Southerland (1906-1994). The young architects established their firm in Tyler, Texas in 1932 and later relocated to Austin. Louis Page, Jr. earned a bachelor's degree in architecture from the University of Texas, a master's degree from the Massachusetts Institute of Technology and attended les Ecoles d'art Américaines de Fontainebleau. Louis Southerland attended the University of Texas before earning his bachelor's degree in architecture at MIT.[15]

PAGE, SOUTHERLAND & PAGE (now PAGE SOUTHERLAND PAGE) was formed when George M. Page (1915-1995) joined Page & Southerland in 1939. He earned his architecture degree from the University of Texas and did post-graduate studies in Europe.[16]

HARVEY L. PAGE (1859-1934), architect, practiced in Washington, D.C. and Chicago before establishing his firm in San Antonio around 1900. Aside from the former Blum's (Frost Bros.) department store, Page's best know surviving San Antonio works are the International & Great Northern Railroad Depot (1907) and Temple Beth-El (1927).[17]

PHELPS & DEWEES (later PHELPS & DEWEES & SIMMONS) was the partnership of San Antonio architects Raymond P. Phelps, Sr. (1890-1958) and Dahl Dewees (1891-1965). Established in 1919, the firm was best known for its institutional buildings, but was probably most influential in its decades-long tenure as supervising architect for the San Antonio school board. C.C. Simmons (1901-1981) graduated from the University of Texas School of Architecture in 1925 and joined the firm as a draftsman; he was made a partner in 1935. Raymond P. Phelps, Jr. (1922-2008) joined his father's firm after graduating from the University of Texas in 1949; he remained in practice until 1993.[18]

HANNIBAL PIANTA (1875-1937), artisan, was born in Boccioletto, Italy. He immigrated to the United States around 1905 and joined his father John in San Antonio. The elder Pianta had been the chief plasterer during construction of the Texas State Capitol and had founded a successful company producing ornamental column capitals. After his father's death in 1912, Hannibal Pianta established his own firm and expanded into modeling and casting art stone architectural ornaments. His sons Eugene, John and Dale later joined him in the family business. The Pianta company modeled and produced the ornamentation for San Antonio's Majestic, Empire and Aztec theaters and Thomas Jefferson High School.[19]

JEREMIAH SCHMIDT (1903-1972), architect, graduated from New Braunfels High School in 1921 and returned to the city after studying at Rice Institute in Houston and at Harvard University. He designed buildings in New Braunfels and nearby towns, and served as an associate architect on projects designed by Austin and San Antonio firms.[20]

EDWARD STEIN (1890-1978), banker and architect, trained at the Armour Institute of Technology in Chicago before returning to Texas to work in his family's business, Stein Lumber Co. He was president of Fredericksburg National Bank when he designed the bank's Art Deco building and created the plans for the modernistic Gillespie County Courthouse.[21]

PEDRO TERÁN, artist and sculptor, was born in Mexico but grew up in San Antonio. He studied art in New Orleans, New York and Chicago before returning to San Antonio to study under José Arpa. Afterward, Terán moved back to Chicago and worked as a freelance artist and designer for Hanns Teichert Studios, where he created sculptures and murals for churches and public buildings across the country. Terán temporarily returned to San Antonio when Teichert Studios won the interior design commission for the Alameda Theater. Although Terán's work was shown regularly at the Art Institute of Chicago and other museums and private galleries, few details are known about his life.[22]

ROY L. THOMAS (1887-1968), architect, attended Southwestern University in Georgetown and the University of Texas at Austin, where he majored in engineering. After working as a draftsman for architects Endress & Walsh, he established his own practice in Austin in 1911. During the 1920s, Thomas designed and supervised construction of several large projects as an associate architect for Sanguinet, Staats & Hedrick. Early in his career Thomas specialized in designing houses; he continued this work in the 1930s when he created his best-known project, the streamlined house of Mr. & Mrs. Herbert Bohn in Austin. Later his practice shifted toward church, school and office design; Thomas created Austin's distinctive Robert E. Lee Elementary School.[23]

ACKNOWLEDGEMENTS

In a project such as this, there are many people to thank and many contributions to be recognized. We are extremely grateful to Ramona Davis, executive director of Greater Houston Preservation Alliance, for her encouragement and support. Ramona was instrumental in the publication of our first book, *Houston Deco*, which made *Hill Country Deco* possible. We also thank the Board of Directors of Greater Houston Preservation Alliance for allowing us to pursue this work, and to Charles D. Maynard, Jr. and Jim Hudson for their guidance.

We offer our sincere appreciation to Mark Wolfe, executive director of the Texas Historical Commission, for graciously contributing the foreword to this book. We are also grateful to architectural historians Stephen Fox and William Seale for their insights.

The Texas Hill Country is home to several outstanding research institutions. We received immeasurable assistance from Patrick Lemelle of the Institute of Texan Cultures, The University of Texas at San Antonio; Bruce MacDougal, Beth Standifird and Rollette Schreckenghost of the San Antonio Conservation Society; Mike Miller, Molly Hults and Grace McEvoy of the Austin History Center, Austin Public Library; Nancy Sparrow of the Alexander Architectural Archives, University of Texas Libraries, The University of Texas at Austin; Beverly Wigley and the volunteers at The Sophienburg Museum and Archives, New Braunfels; Oliver Davis at the Gonzales Memorial Museum; Frank Faulkner and the staff of the Texana/Genealogy Department, San Antonio Public Library; and the volunteers at the Kerr Regional History Center and Archives in Kerrville and the Pioneer Museum/Gillespie County Historical Society in Fredericksburg. Chrysanthe Broikos of the National Building Museum in Washington, D. C. was also very helpful in this endeavor.

Hill Country residents are also fortunate to have access to the services of many outstanding preservation professionals. Our thanks to Leah Brown and Jonathan Poston with the Southwest Office of the National Trust for Historic Preservation; Krista Schreiner Gebbia of Preservation Texas; Michael Holleran of the Graduate Program in Historic Preservation at The University of Texas at Austin; Molly Matthews and Elizabeth Porterfield of the City of San Antonio Historic Preservation Office; Ann McGlone with the City of Alamo Heights; Steve Sadowsky, historic preservation officer for the City of Austin; Jacqui Schraad of the Heritage Society of Austin; Greg Smith with Texas Historical Commission; and Larry Speck of PageSoutherlandPage for their valuable assistance.

This book was made much richer by people who arranged access to otherwise inaccessible historic buildings. Our thanks to Magistrate Judge Andrew W. Austin and David O'Toole of the U. S. Courts Western District of Texas, Austin Division; Dianna Noble and Mark Morales of the Texas Department of Transportation; Anita Fernandez and the staff of Centro Alameda, Inc.; Lane Bourgeois of the U. S. Air Force 12th Flying Training Wing and Robert V. Crawford of the Air Education and Training Command, Randolph Air Force Base; Paula Allen and Ann Marie Bueno of the San Antonio Express-News; and Steve Klein and Patricia Ortiz of the U. S. General Services Administration Greater Southwest Region.

We would also like to thank the individuals who provided us with hard-to-find information or access to privately held historic documents: Phoebe Allen, Florence Baker with First Lutheran Church, Gonzales; Barbara Freidrich with the City of Gonzales Main Street Program; Jean Johnson with the City of Taylor Main Street Program; Lori Moffatt, Anne Cook and Cindy Newsome of *Texas Highways* magazine; Mat Wolff with American Institute of Architects, Houston Chapter; Dustin Fisher of Ebensberger-Fisher Funeral Home in Boerne; Ron Woellhof of Showcase Antiques in Fredericksburg, Peter Flagg Maxon, and Le Ann Wolff.

David Bush would especially like to thank David Crawford for his encouragement and support during this project.

Finally, we offer our sincere appreciation to Judy Alter and the board of TCU Press for recognizing the potential in our proposal and to Susan Petty, Melinda Esco, and Ashley Tambunga of TCU Press for their hard work in making this book a reality.

David Bush and Jim Parsons

ILLUSTRATION CREDITS

HISTORIC PHOTOGRAPHS AND DRAWINGS

Alexander Architectural Archive
University of Texas Libraries, The University of Texas at Austin

Ayres & Ayres Collection
Mistletoe Creamery, San Antonio, TX sheet #4
Meador Motor Co., San Antonio, TX sheet #5
Smith-Young Tower, San Antonio, TX
no sheet #, detail, upper portion
Smith-Young oversized photo
Neisner Bldg., sheet #8
Neisner Bldg., sheet #14

Roy L. Thomas Archival Records
Bohn residence, Austin, TX sheet #3
Bohn residence, Austin, TX sheet #6

Texas Architecture Collection
Adams & Adams, Texas State Highway Bldg., Austin, TX sheet #G-13

Austin History Center, Austin Public Library
CO1032 Austin National Bank, exterior (1930)
CO1071 Austin National Bank, interior (1930)
CO5173 District Courtroom, Travis County Courthouse
CO5177 Travis County Courthouse
ND-48-A023 Austin National Bank (1948)
PICA 04775 Texas Memorial Museum
PICA 06734 Varsity Theater (1936)
PICA 24698 Varsity Theater (1980s)
PICH 06737 C&S Sporting Goods
PICH 07320 Residence for Mr. & Mrs. Herbert Bohn

National Building Museum
S.H. Kress & Co. Collection
1989.13.1.6189 Kress building in San Antonio, TX

San Antonio Conservation Society Foundation
84.267 Alameda Theater, Grand Foyer, photograph
84.273 Alameda Theater, Stage, photograph
Alameda Theater, Houston Street Elevation and Theater Interior-Stage, Renderings from N. Straus Nayfach & Co., Architects.

The Sophienburg Museum and Archives, New Braunfels
PN1334B First National Bank of New Braunfels
PO 130-98A Guaranty State Bank
S20-29 Leo Mendlovitz Department Store

Air Force Art Program Office
1981.203 Navigator
1981.204 Gunner
1981.205 Pilot
1981.206 Bombardier
2009.141 "His First Solo Flight"
2009.143 "Navigators Studying the Stars"

University of Texas at San Antonio, Institute of Texan Cultures
092-0155 Photo of Frost Bros. Store. Courtesy of the San Antonio City Public Service Co.
101-0167 Photo of Berryhill residence. Courtesy of Martha N. Bradley.

Zintgraff Collection, UTSA Institute of Texan Cultures
Courtesy of John and Dela White.
Z-273-A Photo of Jaccard Building
Z-908-1 Photo of Earl Abel's Restaurant
Z-908-5 Photo of General Neon Building
Z-1215-B Photo of Alameda Theater
Z-1304-A Karotkin's Building

ORIGINAL PHOTOGRAPHS

David Bush
1209 Elm Street, 1509 West Woodlawn Avenue, 268 East Lullwood Avenue, A&P Food Store, Alameda Theater, Alamo Cenotaph, Alamo National Building, Alamo Stadium, Arcadia Theater, Austin Daily Tribune Building, Austin Municipal Building, Becker School, Berryhill house, Blackshear School, Blum's, Bohn house, Borden's Creamery, Brauntex Theater, Casino Club Building, Central Catholic High School, Central Fire Station No. 1, Central Power & Light Building, Chapline Building, Ebensberger Funeral Home, Edison High School, Elm Street duplex, First Evangelical Lutheran Church, Frank Bros., Fredericksburg National Bank, Fulton Community Center, Gene Meador Packard, Gillespie County Courthouse, Gilmore Pharmacy, Glosserman Chevrolet, Golden West Master Service Station, Gonzales Auditorium, Gonzales Memorial Museum, Grand-Silver Store, Guadalupe County Courthouse, Guadalupe Theater, Guaranty Finance Co., Guaranty State Bank, Harris murals, Hermann Sons Grand Lodge, Hom-Ond Food Store, Horace Mann Junior High, Humble Oil Service Stations (South Laredo Street, McCullough Avenue), Joske's, Kerrville City Hall, King William house, King's Texaco, Lynn Theater, Memorial Police and Fire Station, Mendlovitz Department Store, Menger Electric Co., Monument Hill, Municipal Auditorium, O.R. Mitchell Motors, Palace Theater (Seguin), Palomino Club,

Pease Veterinary Hospital, Raye Theater, Richter's Bakery, Roberson Hall, Sammie's Place, San Antonio Colored Library, San Antonio Express News Building (exterior), Schreiner Cash Food Store, Seguin Memorial Fire and Police Station, Seguin Municipal Building, Seguin Recreation Building, Smith-Young Tower, Stanley Theater, State Health Building, State Highway Building (exteriors), Teatro Progreso, Texas Theater, Thomas Jefferson High School, Travis County Courthouse, Texas Memorial Museum, U.S. Post Offices (Elgin, Kerrville, Lockhart, Smithville), Van Horn Drug Store No. 1, Victor Stanzel Co., Vocational Agriculture Building, White Laundry Co., Woodlawn Telephone Exchange, Woodlawn Theater.

Jim Parsons

2404 Guadalupe Street, 337 East Lullwood Avenue, Alameda Theater, Alamo Cenotaph, Alamo National Building, Austin Daily Tribune Building, Austin Municipal Building, Bexar County Coliseum, Blum's, Brown Building, Casa de Mexico International Building, Cavin Filling Station, Central Fire Station No. 1, Deason Radio, DePuy house, Fidelity Mortgage Co., Grand-Silver Store, Horace Mann Junior High, Humble Oil Service Station (South Presa Street), Joske's, Lampasas City Hall, Lampasas Junior High School, Mission Drive-In Theater, Nichols duplex, Niesner's, Palace Theater (Georgetown), Plaza Hotel Garage, Power Plant No. 2, Randolph Air Force Base Administration Building, Rita Theater, Robert E. Lee School, S.H. Kress & Co., St. Austin's Catholic Church, San Antonio Express News Building (exterior and interior), San Antonio Public Library, Scarbrough's, Scheffler Service Station, State Highway Building, State Theater, Taylor City Hall, Taylor High School Gymnasium, Taylor Motor Co., Texas Memorial Museum, Texas Power & Light Building, Thomas Jefferson High School, Travis County Courthouse, Travis Park Methodist Youth Building, U.S. Court House, U.S. Post Offices (Giddings, San Antonio), Varsity Theater, William Dean Fausett portraits (Pilot, Navigator, Bombardier, Gunner).

NOTES

INTRODUCTION

1 Patricia Raynor, "Off The Wall: New Deal Post Office Murals," *EnRoute* (Washington, D.C.: Smithsonian National Postal Museum, 1997), vol. 6, no. 5, http://www.postalmuseum.si.edu/resources/6a2q_postalmurals.html (accessed October 1, 2009).

2 Texas Almanac, "City Population History from 1850-2000," http://www.texasalmanac.com/population/population-city-historic.pdf.

3 "1929 Building Smashing All Records," *San Antonio Sunday Light*, November 17, 1929.

4 "Telephone Building to be Elaborate Structure," *San Antonio Sunday Light*, November 10, 1929.

5 "Work on Auditorium to Start Sept. 1," *San Antonio Express*, July 31, 1924.

COMMERCIAL

1 "Kress Store Now Ranks Among City's Finest," *San Antonio Light*, May 17, 1939.

2 "The Legacy: S. H. Kress & Co. Stores," Samuel H. Kress Foundation, http://www.kressfoundation.org/about/legacy.aspx?id=82.

3 "City Buys River Channel Land," *San Antonio Express*, March 16, 1926; "Bowen's Island Gets More Skyscrapers," *San Antonio Sunday Light*, September 26, 1926, sec. 7.

4 "Plaza Garage Cost $200,000," *San Antonio Express*, April 22, 1928, sec. G.

5 Stephen Fox, *Houston Architectural Guide*, 2nd ed. (Houston: Herring Press, 1999).

6 "Many Attend Station Opening," *San Antonio Light*, August 5, 1938.

7 "Packard Agency Has New Home," *San Antonio Sunday Light*, November 17, 1929, sec. 2.

8 "New Building of the San Antonio Express," *San Antonio Express*, Dedication Number, Part I, October 29, 1929.

9 Robert Kolarik, "San Antonio Express-News History, Part 2: A New Century," http://www.mysanantonio.com/about_us/express-news/San_Antonio_Express-News_History_Part_2_A_new_century_.html (accessed September 10, 2009).

10 "Paper From Forest to the Home," *San Antonio Express*, April 20, 1930.

11 "Banks-Alamo National Bank," archival file, Texana/Genealogy Department, San Antonio Public Library.

12 "Alamo National Bank Building (1929)," National Register of Historic Places Nomination Form, October 19, 2005. Texas Historical Commission, Austin.

13 "Throngs Fill Blum Store," *San Antonio Light*, September 21, 1903; "Princess Theater Building Will Be Remodeled for Blum's Store at Cost of $175,224 Announced," *San Antonio Express*, July 7, 1929; "Blum's Opens Large Store on Monday," *San Antonio Light*, August 5, 1930; "$200,000 Paid for Fixtures of Blum Store," *San Antonio Express*, March 15, 1931.

14 Austin National Bank had a long relationship with Page architecture firms. After C. H. Page established his practice in 1895, Austin National Bank was his first major commission. C. H. Page & Brother designed the bank's 1910 building and, as Page Brothers, its 1930 remodeling. Page, Southerland & Page designed Austin National's 1956 motor bank, its 1961 downtown bank and, as PageSoutherlandPage, the bank's 1975 skyscraper. "Austin, Its Architects and Architecture, 1836-1986," Manuscript Records AR.2009.005. Austin History Center, Austin Public Library.

15 "Scarbrough Building," Texas State Historical Marker, 2001. The marker is attached to the Scarbrough Building at 101 West Sixth Street in Austin.

16 "Beauty Paramount in Newest S. A. Structures," *San Antonio Sunday Light*, June 14, 1931, sec. 7.

17 "Plans Completed," *San Antonio Express*, November 9, 1930; "New Braunfels Has Building Activity" and "Store Remodeling at Seguin Planned," *San Antonio Express*, February 14, 1932.

18 "Work on New Plant of Mistletoe Creameries Gets Under Way Here," *San Antonio Express*, April 10, 1933; "Borden's Announces the Formal Opening of the South's Finest Dairy Products Plant," advertisement, *San Antonio Light*, November 1, 1933; "Ayres & Ayres, Architects: An Inventory of their Architectural Drawings, Photographs and Records, 1894-1977," Alexander Architectural Archive, http://www.lib.utexas.edu/apl/aaa/collections.html (accessed September 27, 2009).

19 Gillespie County Historical Society, *Pioneers in God's Hills*, Vol. II (Waco, TX: Eakin Press, 2000).

20 "Community Center is Set Back and Modernized," *San Antonio Express*, April 12, 1936.

21 Alison Beshur, "Schreiner's Closes Its Doors for Good," *The Daily Times* (Kerrville, TX), September 24, 2007.

22 "History of the Olmos Bharmacy," http://www.olmosbharmacy.com/menu/bharh.html (accessed September 15, 2009).

23 *Texas Historic Sites Atlas*, "Brown Building," National Register listing 97000364, http://atlas.thc.state.tx.us/index.asp (accessed October 5, 2009).

24 "Frank Bros. to Spend $70,000 for Remodeling," *San Antonio Express*, July 9, 1939.

25 "The Greater Joske Store as It Will Look in 1939," *San Antonio Sunday Light*, December 4, 1938, sec. 7.

26 Claudia Hazlewood, "West, James Marion," *The Handbook of Texas Online*, http://www.tshaonline.org/handbook/online/ (accessed October 7, 2009); "New Paper in State Capitol," *The Big Spring Daily Herald*, September 13, 1939; "Austin Tribune Has Suspended Publication," *The Port Arthur News*, December 30, 1942; "State Buys Building," *San Antonio Light*, October 3, 1945.

27 "Abel's Place Opens Aug. 15," *San Antonio Sunday Light*, August 10, 1941, sec. 7.

28 "$350,000 Bakery To Be Built," *San Antonio Express*, August 16, 1940; "Richter Bakery Expanding," *San Antonio Light*, November 11, 1965.

29 "Department Store Selects Location," *San Antonio Express*, March 20, 1946.

30 "More for Mexico Casa," *San Antonio Express*, July 27, 1947.

31 "O. R. Mitchell Motors Opens New Building," *San Antonio Express*, June 25, 1950.

32 Jeffrey L. Meikle, *Design in the U. S. A.*, Oxford History of Art series (New York: Oxford University Press, 2005).

THEATERS

1 Rogelio Agrasánchez Jr., *Mexican Movies in the United States* (Jefferson, NC: McFarland & Company, Inc., 2006), 123; "Casa Symbol of Culture," *San Antonio Light*, March 9, 1949; Drawings for Alameda Theater, San Antonio Conservation Society.

2 "Colorful Murals Depict History," *San Antonio Light*, March 9, 1949; "Historical Background on Seven Downtown Theaters in San Antonio." San Antonio Conservation Society and San Antonio Arts Council, 1978.

3 Bea W. W. Avant, "An Interview with Mrs. Charlotte Nayfach Garson on the subject of her late husband N. Straus Nayfach," 1982; Maggie Valentine, *The Show Starts on the Sidewalk: An Architectural History of the Movie Theatre*, Starring S. Charles Lee (New Haven: Yale University Press, 1996), 205; The UCLA Digital Library, "Chapultepec Theatre," http://digital.library.ucla.edu/sclee/servlet/SCLeeServlet (accessed October 7, 2009); "N. S. Nayfach Rites Slated," *San Antonio Light*, June 16, 1948.

4 "Theatre Designer Dies at Dallas," *Big Spring Daily Herald* (TX), October 20, 1937.

5 *Texas General Contractors Association Monthly Bulletin*, April 1935 (Houston: Texas General Contractors Association) and Howard Theater Web Site (www.howardtheatre.com/history.htm).

6 Corgan Associates, "Our Story," http://www.corgan.com/#/profile/ourstory (accessed October 3, 2009).

7 John Eberson Collection, The Architectural Archives of The University Pennsylvania, http://www.philadelphiabuildings.org/faids/aaup/Eberson.pdf.

8 "New Shrine for Hill Country Movie Fans," June 24, 1926; "Arcadia Remodeling To Cost $100,000, Completed In August," *Kerrville Mountain Sun*, April 8, 1948.

RESIDENTIAL

1 Marsia Hart Reese, "A Vision of Shangri-La," *Austin Homes & Gardens*, April 1982, 38-45.

2 "Bohns Observe Golden Anniversary," *Austin Statesman*, June 1, 1942; "Bohn Bros. 47 Years Ago! – Bohn Bros. Today!" advertisement, *Austin Statesman*, March 26, 1939.

3 National Register of Historic Places Registration Form, "Herbert and Alice Bohn House," February 17, 1997, Texas Historical Commission.

4 Heritage Society of Austin, Heritage Homes Tour docent script, May 1995; National Register, "Herbert and Alice Bohn House."

5 *Texas Almanac*, "City Population History."

6 National Register, "Herbert and Alice Bohn House."

7 "San Antonio Turns to Modernistic Homes," *San Antonio Light*, February 2, 1936; "San Antonio Home Recognized," *San Antonio Express*, November 11, 1936.

8 "Pilon," *San Antonio Light*, March 14, 1938.

INSTITUTIONAL

1 Travis County Archives, "The Travis County Courthouse," http://www.traviscountyhistory.org/courthouse.html (accessed October 4, 2009).

2 Jason Scott Smith, *Building New Deal Liberalism: the Political Economy of Public Works*, 1933-1956 (New York: Cambridge University Press, 2006), 88; Nick Taylor, *American-Made: The Enduring Legacy of the WPA* (New York: Random House, 2009).

3 C. W. Short and R. Stanley-Brown, *Public Buildings: Architecture Under the Public Works Administration*, 1933-39, Vol. 1 (Cambridge, Mass.: Da Capo Press, 1986); Raynor, "Off The Wall: New Deal Post Office Murals."

4 Seguin Area Chamber of Commerce, "Demographics & Community Profile," http://www.seguinchamber.com/1773768_14214.htm (accessed October 4, 2009); *Seguin, Texas City Directory* (Detroit: R. L. Polk & Co., 1938), 5.

5 *Texas Historic Sites Atlas*, "San Antonio Casino Club Building," National Register listing 80004078, http://atlas.thc.state.tx.us/index.asp (accessed September 30, 2009).

6 "The Aztec, $1,500,000 Theater, Will Be Ready for 1926 Season," *San Antonio Express*, May 31, 1925.

7 *Texas Historic Sites Atlas*, "Carver, George Washington, Library and Auditorium," National Register listing 301162, http://atlas.thc.state.tx.us/index.asp (accessed October 3, 2009).

8 *Texas Historic Sites Atlas*, "Base Administration Building-Randolph AFB," National Register listing 87001434, "Randolph Field Historic District," National Register listing 9600753, http://atlas.thc.state.tx.us/index.asp (accessed October 5, 2009); "U. S. Air Force Fact Sheet: Taj Mahal," Randolph Air Force Base, http://www.randolph.af.mil/library/factsheets/ (accessed September 30, 2009); "Architects Rush Plans for San Antonio Army Buildings," *San Antonio Sunday Light*, February 9, 1930; "Building 100," Texas State Historical Marker, 1975. The marker is located on the north lawn of the building.

9 "U. S. Fliers Inspire Randolph Field Mural," *San Antonio Sunday Light*, March 12, 1944; "Randolph Field Murals Accepted Saturday After 17 Months' Work," *San Antonio Express*, March 12, 1944.

10 Robert Goetz, "Taj Mahal's senior inhabitants gone for now, but will be back as good as new," *Air Force Print News Today*, July 24, 2009.

11 "Pictorial Magazine to Feature School," *San Antonio Light*, October 31, 1937; "Jefferson Girls in Fox Newsreel," *San Antonio Light*, April 25, 1938.

12 Thomas Jefferson High School Historical Preservation Society, "History of Thomas Jefferson High School," http://tjhps.com/history.htm (accessed October 4, 2009).

13 "Construction Set to Begin Monday on New City Hall, *Kerrville Mountain Sun*, February 11, 1937.

14 Hermann Sons Fraternal Insurance, "History," http://www.texashermannsons.org/?page=history (accessed October 4, 2009).

15 Lila Knight, from "Texas 50," *Texas Architect*, (Nov./Dec. 1989), 52.

16 Antoinette J. Lee, *Architects to the Nation*, 258-260.

17 "10 Nurses Finish Hospital Course," *San Antonio Express*, May 13, 1939.

18 Raynor, "Off The Wall: New Deal Post Office Murals."

19 Philip Parisi, *The Texas Post Office Murals: Art for the People* (College Station: Texas A&M University Press, 2004); U. S. General Services Administration, "Hipolito F. Garcia Federal Building and U. S. Courthouse, San Antonio, TX," http://www.gsa.gov/Portal/gsa/ep/channelView.do?pageTypeId=17109&channelId=-24364 (accessed October 12, 2009).

20 "New Stadium 79th for WPA," *San Antonio Express*, September 2, 1040.

21 "Century of Sports Depicted in Murals at Alamo Stadium," *San Antonio Express*, April 24, 1941.

22 W. G. Etheridge, "Texas Trails," *San Antonio Light*, September 2, 1940.

23 "Ground Is Broken For New Texas Health Building," *The Galveston Daily News*, March 10, 1942; "Fourth Floor Being Added to State Health Building," *Amarillo Globe*, August 17, 1948. Anson Jones Building/Avenue Lofts Condominiums Building Documentation & Nomination Form, Heritage Society of Austin 2007 Preservation Awards.

24 *Austin City Connection*, "Seaholm District History," http://www.ci.austin.tx.us/seaholm/history.htm (accessed October 2, 2009).

25 "Travis Park Church Building Program Set, *San Antonio Express*, June 27, 1948; "Travis Park to Dedicate New Building," *San Antonio Express*, January 4, 1950.

COMMEMORATIVE

1 *The Handbook of Texas Online*, "Texas Memorial Museum," http://www.tshaonline.org/handbook/online/index.html (accessed October 6, 2009).

2 "Million-Dollar Texas Memorial Museum," *The Galveston Daily News*, February 1, 1936; University of Texas Campus Tours, "Paul Philippe Cret (1876-1945)," http://www.utexas.edu/tours/mainbuilding/people/cret.html (accessed October 6, 2009); "Texas Memorial Museum Nears Opening," *San Antonio Express*, December 18, 1938.

3 Carol Morris Little, *A Comprehensive Guide to Outdoor Sculpture in Texas* (Austin: University of Texas Press, 1996), 312; "Coppini, Commemorator," *The Rotarian*, October 1939, 47.

4 James Wright Steely, *Parks for Texas: Enduring Landscapes of the New Deal* (Austin: University of Texas Press, 1999), 219; Carol Morris Little, *A Comprehensive Guide to Outdoor Sculpture*, 312; *The Handbook of Texas Online*, "Dawson Massacre," (by Thomas W. Cutrer), "Black Bean Episode," http://www.tshaonline.org/handbook/online/index.html (accessed October 2, 2009).

5 "Gonzales Gets $54,000 Museum," *San Antonio Express*, December 20, 1936.

6 "Alamo Defenders Honored At Joint Armistice Day-Cenotaph Dedication Rites," *San Antonio Express*, November 12, 1940.

7 "Ground to be Broken Next Week for $100,000 Alamo Cenotaph, State Board Accepts Model," *San Antonio Express*, March 7, 1939.

ARCHITECTS AND ARTISTS

1 Ellis A. Davis, "Carleton W. Adams," *New Encyclopedia of Texas* (Dallas: Texas Development Bureau, 1929), 755.

2 "Paper From Forest to the Home," *San Antonio Express*, April 20, 1930; "Early Texas Artists: José Arpa," http://www.harryhalff.com/jose.htm (accessed October 3, 2009).

3 "Ayres and Ayres Architects: An Inventory of their Architectural Drawings, Photographs and Records, 1894-1977," Alexander Architectural Archive, http://www.lib.utexas.edu/apl/aaa/collections.html (accessed October 1, 2009).

4 "The Texas Exposition," *Daily Capital News* (Jefferson City, MO), November 12, 1936; "Fair Park, TX: Art and Architecture Fact Sheet," http://www.dallascityhall.com/FairPark/fair_park_factsheet.html (accessed October 3, 2009); "Pierre Bourdelle Mural," http://barrickmurals.blogspot.com/2009/02/mural-by-pierre-bourdelle-actually.html (accessed October 3, 2009)

5 Stephanie Hetos Cocke, "Cocke, Bartlett," *The Handbook of Texas Online*, http://www.tshaonline.org/handbook/online/index.html (accessed September 30, 2009)

6 *The Handbook of Texas Online*, "Coppini, Pompeo Luigi," http://www.tshaonline.org/handbook/online/index.html (accessed September 29, 2009).

7 *Texas Historic Sites Atlas*, "Norwood Tower," Historical Marker 13620, http://atlas.thc.state.tx.us/index.asp (accessed October 1, 2009); Jim Parsons and David Bush, *Houston Deco: Modernistic Architecture of the Texas Coast* (Albany, TX: Bright Sky Press, 2008).

8 *Texas Historic Sites Atlas*, "Lee, Robert E., Hotel," National Register listing 95000063, http://atlas.thc.state.tx.us/index.asp (accessed September 30, 2009).

9 "Harris, Ethel Wilson, House," National Register of Historic Places narrative description (2001), NR reference number 1000325; Steve Bennett, "Tile artists captured city's essence," *San Antonio Express-News*, September 13, 2009.

10 "The Kelwood Co. Praises Monte Vista," advertisement, *San Antonio Express*, April 27, 1924; "The Kelwood Co.," advertisement, *San Antonio Express*, April 27, 1924; *Texas Historic Sites Atlas*, "Aztec Theater," National Register listing 92001403, "Bushnell," National Register listing 82004491, http://atlas.thc.state.tx.us/index.asp (accessed September 29, 2009).

11 Hank Todd Smith, ed., *Austin: Its Architects and Architecture, 1836-1936*, (Austin: Austin Chapter, American Institute of Architects, 1986), 13; "Santa Rita Courts," National Register of Historic Place registration form, http://www.flma.org/santarita/Santa%20Rita%20Nomination.pdf (accessed October 2, 2009); Obituary of R. Max Brooks, *The New York Times*, September 11, 1982.

12 "Hugo F. Kuehne," *Bulletin of the University of Texas*, No. 166, Vol. 10, No. 3, January 8, 1911; Roxanne Williamson, "Kuehne, Hugo Franz," *The Handbook of Texas Online*, http://www.tshaonline.org/handbook/online/index.html (accessed September 30, 2009).

13 "An interview with Mrs. Charlotte Nayfach Garson on the subject of her late husband N. Straus Nayfach," by Bea W.W. Avant, June 1982, transcript; Charlotte Nayfach Garson interview by Dwayne Jones, June 21, 1995, transcript; N. Straus Nayfach file, San Antonio Conservation Society.

14 Roxanne Williamson, "Page, Charles Henry," *The Handbook of Texas Online*, http://www.tshaonline.org/handbook/online/index.html (accessed September 29, 2009); Jay C. Henry, *Architecture in Texas, 1895-1945* (Austin: University of Texas Press, 1993); Michael Andrews, *Historic Texas Courthouses* (Albany, TX: Bright Sky Press, 2006); Obituary of Charles H. Page, Jr., *The Paris (TX) News*, March 31, 1998.

15 "Austin, Its Architects and Architecture, 1836-1986," Manuscript Records AR.2009.005, Austin History Center, Austin Public Library.

16 Hank Todd Smith, *Austin: Its Architects and Architecture*.

17 Christopher Long, "Page, Harvey Lindsley," *The Handbook of Texas Online*, http://www.tshaonline.org/handbook/online/index.html (accessed October 6, 2009).

18 "Architects for School Building Program Named," *San Antonio Express*, August 22, 1922; "School Board Spending Plan Slated," *San Antonio Light*, June 7, 1955; "Architect Phelps Dies," *San Antonio Light*, October 9, 1958; "Colonel Simmons, architect, dies," San Antonio Public Library Texana/Genealogy Department, Archival Files, Obituaries-1981; "Phelps, 86, remembered for architectural landmarks throughout Texas," *San Antonio Express-News*, December 1, 2008.

19 "Pianta's Business Steadily Grows," *San Antonio Express*, September 1, 1924; "Hannibal Pianta, Master Modeler," http://www.battersbyornamental.com/pianta.htm (accessed October 1, 2009).

20 Max Schmidt (brother of Jeremiah Schmidt), 1995 interview, transcript, New Braunfels Sesquicentennial file, The Sophienburg Museum and Archives, New Braunfels, TX.

21 Gillespie County Historical Society, *Pioneers of God's Hills*, Vol. II (Waco: Eakin Press, 2005); Obituary for Edward Stein, Sr., Kerrville Mountain Sun, April 27, 1978.

22 "The Alameda Theater: historical background" compiled by Bea W.W. Avant, July 1982, theater file, San Antonio Conservation Society.

23 Christopher Long, "Thomas, Roy Leonidas," *The Handbook of Texas Online*, http://www.tshaonline.org/handbook/online/index.html (accessed September 29, 2009).

BIBLIOGRAPHY

Andrews, Michael. *Historic Courthouses of Texas*. Albany, TX: Bright Sky Press, 2006.

Breeze, Carla. American Art Deco: *Modernistic Architecture and Regionalism*. New York: W. W. Norton and Company, Inc., 2003.

Federal Writers' Project of the Work Projects Administration in the State of Texas, Warren E. Gettys, director. *San Antonio: A History and Guide*. New York: Hastings House, 1941.

Federal Writers' Project of the Work Projects Administration in the State of Texas, Warner E. Gettys, director. *Texas: A Guide to the Lone Star State*. New York: Hastings House, 1940.

Fox, Stephen. *Houston Architectural Guide*. 2nd ed. Houston: Herring Press, 1999.

Frampton, Kenneth. *Modern Architecture: A Critical History*. 3rd ed. London: Thames and Hudson, Ltd., 1992.

Gambino, Carol Newton and David Halpern. *Tulsa Art Deco*. Tulsa, OK: Tulsa Architecture Foundation, 2001.

Henry, Jay C. *Architecture in Texas, 1895-1945*. Austin: University of Texas Press, 1993.

Keahy, Kirby and Allen McCree, eds. *Austin and its Architecture*. Austin Chapter American Institute of Architects and Women's Architecture League, 1976.

Lee, Antoinette J. *Architects to the Nation: The Rise and Decline of the Supervising Architect's Office*. New York: Oxford University Press, 2000.

Parisi, Philip. *The Texas Post Office Murals: Art for the People*. College Station: Texas A&M University Press, 2004.

Short, C. W. and R. Stanley-Brown. *Public Buildings: Architecture Under the Public Works Administration, 1933-39*. New York: Da Capo Press, Inc., 1986.

Smith, Hank Todd, ed. *Austin: Its Architects and Architecture (1836-1986)*. Austin Chapter American Institute of Architects, 1986.

Texas General Contractors Association Monthly Bulletin. Various issues. Houston: Texas General Contractors Association, 1926-1937.

Four Web sites were particularly useful in researching this book:

http://atlas.thc.state.tx.us/ Texas Historical Commission's online *Texas Historic Sites Atlas* includes data on Texas properties listed in the National Register of Historic Places and information from state historical markers.

http://www.tsha.utexas.edu/handbook/online/ Texas Historical Association's *Handbook of Texas Online* contains biographies of significant individuals, including architects, builders and business men, as well as accounts of important events in Texas history.

http://www.lib.utexas.edu/apl/aaa/ *Alexander Architectural Archive*, University of Texas Libraries, The University of Texas at Austin, includes concise biographical information about a number of architects; the online catalog of architectural drawings sorts building documentation by architect.

http://www.newspaperarchive.com/ NewspaperARCHIVE.com proved invaluable for quickly locating information in regional newspapers of the period. The San Antonio newspapers, in particular, provided a treasure trove of information that included renderings of many of the buildings in this book, historic names of buildings, architects' names and completion dates.

INDEX

ABOUT THIS BOOK

Designed by Richard Whittington/Whittington & Co., Austin, Texas

Printed and bound by Everbest Printing Co. through Four Colour Imports, Ltd., Louisville, Kentucky

Composed in Memphis text, typeface designed by Rudolf Wolf in 1930. The display typeface is Neutraface Titling designed by Christian Schwartz in 2002.

Printed on 93# Gold East Matte Art paper

Bound in JHT Cloth

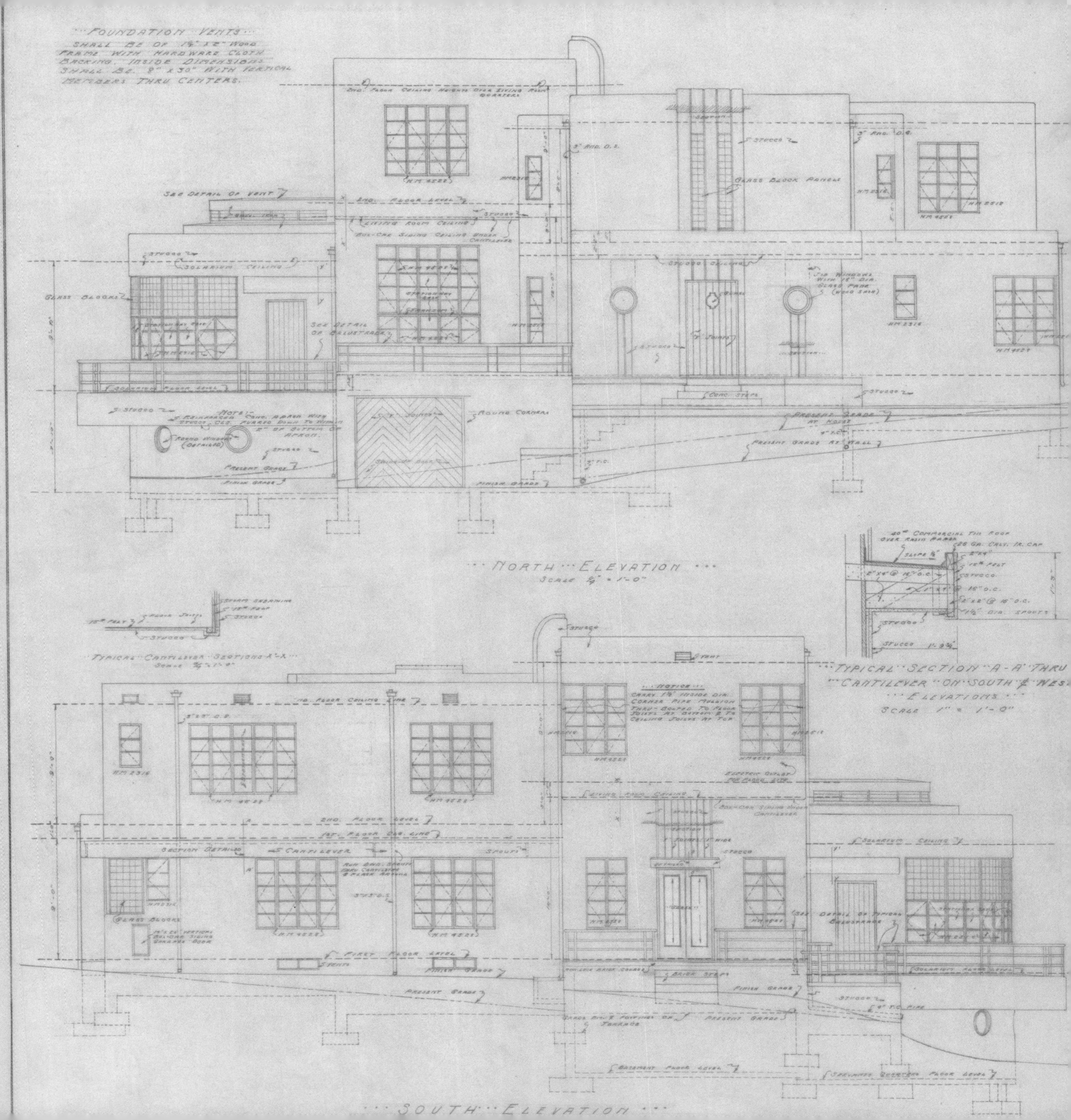
FOUNDATION VENTS
SHALL BE OF 1¾" x 2" WOOD FRAME WITH HARDWARE CLOTH BACKING. INSIDE DIMENSIONS SHALL BE 8" x 30" WITH VERTICAL MEMBERS THRU CENTERS.
NORTH ELEVATION
SCALE ¼" = 1'-0"
TYPICAL CANTILEVER SECTIONS X-X
TYPICAL SECTION "A-A" THRU CANTILEVER ON SOUTH & WEST ELEVATIONS
SCALE 1" = 1'-0"
SOUTH ELEVATION